Multimedia Systems

Springer

London
Berlin
Heidelberg
New York
Barcelona
Hong Kong
Milan
Paris
Singapore
Tokyo

The Springer-Verlag Series on Applied Computing is an advanced series of innovative textbooks that span the full range of topics in applied computing technology.

Books in the series provide a grounding in theoretical concepts in computer science alongside real-world examples of how those concepts can be applied in the development of effective computer systems.

The series should be essential reading for advanced undergraduate and postgraduate students in computing and information systems.

Books in this series are contributed by international specialist researchers and educators in applied computing who draw together the full range of issues in their specialist area into one concise authoritative textbook.

Titles already available:

Deryn Graham and Anthony Barrett
Knowledge-Based Image Processing Systems
3–540–76027-X

Derrick Morris, Gareth Evans, Peter Green, Colin Theaker
Object Orientated Computer Systems Engineering
3–430–76020-2

John Hunt
Java and Object Orientation: An Introduction
3–540–76148-9

David Gray
Introduction to the Formal Design of Real-Time Systems
3–540–76140-3

Mike Holcombe and Florentin Ipate
Correct Systems: Building A Business Process Solution
3–540–76246-9

Jan Noyes and Chris Baber
User-Centred Design of Systems
3–540–76007-5

Arturo Trujillo
Translation Engines: Techniques for Machine Translation
1–85233–057-0

Ulrich Nehmzow
Mobile Robotics: A Practical Introduction
1–85233–173-9

Fabio Paternò
Model-Based Design and Evaluation of Interactive Applications
1–85233–155-0

Tim Morris

Multimedia Systems

Delivering, Generating and Interacting with Multimedia

 Springer

Tim Morris, BSc PhD
Department of Computation, UMIST, PO Box 88, Manchester,
M60 1QD, UK

Series Editors
Professor Ray J. Paul, BSc MSc PhD
Dean of the Faculty of Science, Brunel University, Uxbridge, Middlesex UB8 3PH, UK
Professor Peter J. Thomas, MIEE MBCS CEng FRSA
Centre for Personal Information Management, University of the West of England,
Frenchay Campus, Bristol BS16 1QY, UK
Dr Jasna Kuljis, PhD MS Dipl Ing
Department of Information Systems and Computing, Brunel University,
Uxbridge, Middlesex UB8 3PH, UK

ISBN 1-85233-248-4 Springer-Verlag London Berlin Heidelberg

British Library Cataloguing in Publication Data
Morris, Tim
   Multimedia systems : delivering, generating, and interacting
   with multimedia - (Applied computing)
   1. Multimedia systems. 2. Interactive multimedia
   I. Title
   006.7

   ISBN 1-85233-248-4
Library of Congress Cataloging-in-Publication Data
Morris, Tim, 1960-
   Multimedia systems : delivering, generating, and
   interacting with multimedia / Tim Morris.
      p. cm. -- (Applied computing)
   Includes bibliographical references and index.
   ISBN 1852332484 (alk. paper)
   1. Multimedia systems. I. Title. II. Series.
QA76.575. M665 2000
006.7-dc21   00-037377

© Springer-Verlag London Limited 2000
Printed in Great Britain

Typesetting: Florence Production Ltd, Stoodleigh, Devon
Printed and bound by Athenæum Press, Gateshead, Tyne & Wear
34/3830-543210 Printed on acid-free paper SPIN 10749452

Preface

What are Multimedia Systems?

This book is intended to expose you to multimedia in its widest sense. The popular understanding of this subject is that it is the integration and delivery of text, images and sound, usually on a desktop PC. We are all familiar with examples from the extensive range of multimedia titles available on CD-ROM. These give us a rich set of sensory experiences, and, perhaps more important, we are free to navigate our way through the information as we choose. However, this is only half of the story since these titles can only *deliver* information.

A recent IEEE publication (Chen, 1997) suggested that multimedia should include all systems that integrate diverse media, in standalone or networked applications, either for presentation or communication. Diverse media implies visual and aural information (text, static and moving pictures and sound). Networking could be realised using intranet or telephone links. Presentation systems would imply the multimedia delivery systems with which we are all familiar. Communication implies a two-way interaction with the computer. So as well as transmitting information, multimedia systems should also be able to understand and react to information presented to them using the same set of diverse media (such as typed text, pictures and sound).

The aims of this book are therefore twofold:

1. to introduce the methods of generating, manipulating and delivering multimedia data;
2. to give an overview of current research that will illustrate what tasks multimedia systems will soon be achieving in the realm of human and computer interaction.

Multimedia Delivery Systems

A multimedia delivery system can be any computer system capable of presenting multimedia information. This implies that the computer system has a graphics subsystem that is able to display high resolution images and also has a throughput rate sufficiently high to present moving images on screen. The computer system will also have a sound subsystem whose throughput requirements are less demanding but must nevertheless deliver realistic sound data. At one time this would have meant a computer system with significant hardware additions, at present, an entry-level computer is likely to have these capabilities.

The delivery system must also have some means of receiving input from the operator. Typically this will be via a keyboard or mouse, but voice input is becoming more common.

The delivery system will be of limited use without data to deliver and the software to drive it. The archetype example is the CD-ROM. A CD may contain a game, an encyclopaedia, a travel guide or any other data, plus the software to browse that data. More esoteric examples can be found. A national chain of supermarkets has a computer system with which customers are able to browse a small database of recipes and vouchers. A local transport authority has a publicly accessible information booth that provides data regarding bus routes and timetables. Systems such as these two have very different hardware requirements to a computer system that is to sit on a desk in the home, classroom or office. But these systems also have the same delivery characteristics as a desktop system: the user has some control over what data he is presented and how he is able to navigate through the available information.

Multimedia Interactivity

All multimedia systems are interactive to a certain, limited, degree. If this were not so then we would be unable to navigate a path through the data. However, the currently available multimedia systems have extremely limited channels of interactivity. Typically, we may use the mouse, keyboard or perhaps voice input to control the system. The systems themselves are also limited, the majority being desktop PCs, with some exceptions. A major strand in this book will be to examine novel multimedia interactions. The single outstanding characteristic of these systems is that they allow communication from the computer user to the computer to be via any more natural channel that the mouse or keyboard. This could be using voice control, using gestures, by the computer "reading" sign language or lips. Example systems are being developed by most major hardware and software manufacturing corporations, whether this is to control domestic appliances, to simplify office work patterns or to deliver information on the shop floor.

The look and feel of the computer is also changing. If the aim of developing multimedia interactivity is to facilitate human/computer interaction, then the computer can be removed from the desktop and there may be no need for a mouse or keyboard, or perhaps even the screen. Ultimately, using the multimedia computer will seem as natural as talking to a friend.

Course Background

This book was developed for a single semester course of the same name given to advanced undergraduate and postgraduate students in the Department of Computation at UMIST. None of the students who attend the course has had any previous exposure to courses dealing with multimedia systems. Although some students have attended modules dealing with computer vision, computer graphics or speech understanding, these are not prerequisites for the course which is entirely self contained.

The course has been delivered using a mixture of formal lectures, tutorials and assessed exercises over a period of 12 weeks. Some of the students attending the course have a stronger background in mathematics than others. Rather than exclude any because of their prior knowledge, the specialist topics required by the course are presented in appendices.

The Book's Organisation

My intention in this book is to do more than equip students to design multimedia delivery systems. I also intend to outline what multimedia computers could be doing five years from now. Therefore the book is divided into two parts. Part I (Chapters 2 to 4) will discuss how multimedia delivery systems are designed and constructed. The description is necessarily brief and the interested reader is referred to more specialist books on each topic. Part II (Chapters 5 to 11) will discuss methods of realising true multimedia computing; hence the book's subtitle: generating and interacting with multimedia.

Part I starts with an examination of human perception and data coding (see Chapter 1). The rationale for this is that if we are to present information in a pleasing and realistic fashion, then we ought to be able to specify what pleasing and realistic actually mean. In perceptual terms, this implies that we must examine the typical human's ability to see images and video and to hear sound to find what is the resolution of our visual and aural systems. This then dictates the resolution we must have for the images, videos and sounds that our multimedia systems must deliver if they are to look realistic. Methods of storing these objects are also examined.

The next chapter presents an examination of the methods with which multimedia delivery systems are assembled. How is the raw data organised and how is the reader's path through the data facilitated? The first half of the book concludes with an examination of the hardware used in multimedia systems, what are the requirements of a multimedia computer and what peripheral devices are required to capture, manipulate and present multimedia data. The typical multimedia computer is presented, along with alternatives and their areas of application.

The second half of the book examines a number of topics, most of which are still based in the laboratory, some of which are beginning to appear as commercial products. These are perceptual interfaces. They include systems able to understand human speech, systems able to synthesise speech, systems able to observe the user's eyes and interpret direction of gaze as a command to move the cursor, systems able to recognise and interpret gestures made by the user and systems able to respond to completely unconstrained input. In short, the input to these systems is via any channel other than the keyboard or mouse. A chapter is devoted to each topic. The penultimate chapter is concerned with the generation of visual feedback. In the same way as speech synthesis was examined as a method of providing aural feedback, visual feedback is necessary is particular systems.

The book has several appendices that contain information that is useful but not directly relevant to the course. An overview of HTML (hypertext mark-up language) is presented. This is useful as it is a vehicle for presenting multimedia systems and has been used by students following the course in designing websites as an assessed exercise. The overview is necessarily brief and the reader must be referred to other texts for a more complete description. All of the specialist mathematical techniques are described in a second appendix. Finally, a discussion of some publicly available software is given, this is restricted to relevant software that will manipulate images, sounds and video sequences.

Supplementary Materials

The text is supplemented by information available on an associated website: www.co.umist.ac.uk/~dtm/software.html. This material includes transparencies and source material used in assessments.

Bibliography

Tsuhan Chen (1997) The past, present and future of multimedia signal processing. IEEE Signal Processing 14.

Contents

1 Introduction

What are Multimedia Systems?

Multimedia has become an extremely powerful selling point in today's home computer market. But what is "multimedia"? And is there more to this subject than the advertising hype would suggest?

A "multimedia computer" has come to mean a personal computer capable of displaying high-quality digital images, and playing digital sound and digital video with a satisfactory degree of realism. A suitable computer may have many potential uses, in education, business, industry, medicine and not least in entertainment.

In education, the ability of the multimedia computer to present information in a flexible and interesting manner has been exploited in developing materials for delivering the curriculum. The material is designed such that students are able to study independently, following their own interests (within the curriculum's constraints) and at their own pace. A major strength of providing computerised materials is that the expertise of the teacher is potentially available simultaneously to all of the students on an individual basis. This also has advantages in that the curriculum can be delivered automatically, leaving the teacher to concentrate on other time demanding tasks.

In business, multimedia applications have been used to visualise data and their inter-relationships. This has been of use in regulating the supply of goods and services, in visualising the structure of organisations, and so on.

An interesting example comes from the field of aircraft maintenance, where service manuals are available online to be browsed by the maintenance staff as they are working using a portable computer. Providing the information in a multimedia format is not novel, what is original in this application is that the computer is small enough to be worn on a belt-pack and the display is head mounted. The service engineer can then view the service manual as he or she is working on the aircraft.

Similar examples could be imagined in medicine, where a surgeon may choose to refer to online information during the course of an operation. Whilst this application could be imagined, it has not yet been implemented, for a range of practical and professional reasons. However, multimedia systems are finding applications in informing and training; informing the public of health issues and training doctors and surgeons. One of the more interesting examples is training surgeons in the use of keyhole surgery, once this was "on the job training", then simulators were used that mocked-up the abdomen, latterly the mechanical simulators have been replaced by software simulations in which the endoscope view is displayed and the manipulators are provided with tactile feedback.

The entertainment field provides the largest number and most familiar examples of multimedia systems. It is probably true that the home entertainment market has been one of the largest driving forces behind the development of affordable multimedia systems. This has occurred to such an extent that we now have many different types of peripheral device specifically for the home computer, for example, steering wheels and car-like pedals for interfacing to racing car simulators. It is also probably true that using the home computer for entertainment is its single largest use in some age groups.

The rapid development of the personal computer has facilitated these applications. Not many years ago, playing sound and video data would have required extremely expensive additional hardware since a standard desktop computer simply did not have the processing power to do these things. This hardware would have included additional storage, an additional graphics processor, a sound card and possibly a video decoder. Today, however, it is almost impossible to buy a desktop computer that is not capable of playing multimedia data. The typical home or workplace computer is now able to:

1. play sound with CD quality i.e. as good as is necessary for the sound to be of acceptable quality;
2. play video clips at broadcast quality without needing an additional video processor;
3. render graphical images with a high degree of realism within tolerable time spans;
4. render complex graphical scenes rapidly, giving the appearance of real-time motion through a virtual environment.

The ability to play multimedia data is a basic requirement for many of today's computer applications. The single characteristic of all of these multimedia applications is the integration and delivery of diverse data types. The application naturally uses the keyboard and mouse to receive information from the user, but is not restricted to using text to convey information to the user, rather the text is augmented by images, videos and sound clips.

But if our understanding of multimedia is restricted to the rendering of data on a desktop computer, we will have a very poor appreciation of the depth and breadth of this subject. In addition, multimedia should be understood to include the development of hardware and software that creates, manipulates or transmits more than one data type. The topic will include the multimedia we have experienced at home, but will also include human–computer interaction, manipulation of data types other than simple text and the vast range of applications that can make use of these technologies.

Some of these applications have already become available. They are still characterised by their delivery of multimedia, but most also include some data capture. For example, videoconferencing used to require dedicated communication channels and studio facilities, but with the advent of cheap digital cameras, the desktop computer can become a videoconferencing studio. The conferencing application still does very little in the way of sophisticated processing, it limits itself to capturing sound and image data, encoding, transmitting, receiving, decoding and displaying it. Whilst this is a significant improvement for communication between distant parties, it is still a conceptually simple application that has much scope for improvement. Similarly, applications exist that can capture and encode video data, in real time, and broadcast it over wide area networks, major terrestrial television news channels offer this service.

One of the more significant multimedia achievements has been speech understanding. Results of the first investigations into the problem were reported in the 1970s. Shortly afterwards the American DARPA (Defence Advanced Research Project Agency) announced a 5 year initiative whose goal was to deliver software systems capable of comprehending the natural speech of any individuals. It is a testimony to the complexity of the problem, that at the end of the 5 year programme, despite the involvement of major research institutions, the problem remained unsolved. The more advanced systems that were developed were only capable of decoding isolated words. It was only some 15 years later that IBM and others began to market what were essentially computerised dictation machines, but are able to decode continuously spoken words.

Other methods of human computer interaction have been suggested, some are being actively researched, others remain ideas for future work. Much current research is directed towards finding ways of emulating human communication. For example, if the problem of understanding speech can be solved, it must also be possible to discover how to lipread, to understand gestures or sign language. The response of *HAL*, the computer in *2001: A Space Odyssey* may not be far off, when it was asked "how did you know we were talking?" *HAL* replied, "I saw your lips move, Dave".

So far in this introduction, multimedia systems have been presented as those systems that deliver multimedia data, or enable multimedia communication between the computer and a human operator. A recent IEEE report suggested that the subject should include these topics, plus the enabling technologies. Specifically, multimedia systems could encompass:

• Multimedia processing of text, speech, music, images, graphics, and video.
• Interaction among multimedia representations of signals.
• Compression, manipulation, and interactive access of multimedia signals.
• Human-computer interfaces, intelligent agents.
• Human and machine perception: audio, visual, and multi-modality.
• Applications: distant learning, tele-medicine, home-shopping, virtual reality, games.
• Databases: video-on-demand, digital library, multimedia servers.
• Multimedia communication: transport, synchronisation, protocols.
• Network issues: wireless, ATM, packet audio-visual services.
• VLSI implementation: architectures, audio/video codecs, low-power circuits.
• Standards: DAVIC, Java, MHEG, JPEG, MPEG, VRML.
• Emerging technologies: Internet, WWW, hypertext, and hypermedia.

The traditional view of multimedia introduced above, encompasses only a very small portion of the whole subject. In turn, the subject covers a wider range of topics than will be addressed in this book. Briefly, the book will discuss how multimedia delivery systems are designed and assembled, and how new approaches to multimedia interactivity are bearing fruit.

Multimedia Delivery Systems

A multimedia delivery system can be considered as any computer system designed to play multimedia data files, be they sounds, images, graphics, video clips or simple text. The system will also allow its user to navigate a path through the data. Such a system is typical of the "traditional" (if such a new phenomenon can have traditions!) examples of multimedia such as the programmes used for home entertainment, and the widespread educational software. The world wide web could also be considered as a multimedia delivery system.

A multimedia delivery system will have three fundamental components: the hardware hosting the system, the software delivering the content and the content itself. An appreciation of all components and their mutual relationships is necessary for the design of effective multimedia.

The data being presented by the multimedia system will include some or all of the different types of multimedia. The implementer of a multimedia system should be aware of the human perception of these elements in order to be assured of the quality of the data being presented. For example, it is useful to know the rate above which individual frames of an image sequence blur into continuous motion.

Developing multimedia titles is seldom the work of one person alone, software engineers and graphic designers will all be involved. Nevertheless, the design and implementation process will pass through well defined stages, and certain well documented models can be used in the design. These models will be examined.

It was stated above, that it would be difficult to purchase a home or workplace computer that was not suitable for use as a multimedia computer. Five years ago this was not the case. The designer of multimedia delivery systems must be aware of the hardware that is used in today's home computers, what alternatives are available and where those alternatives would be best used.

Multimedia Interactivity

Interactive multimedia systems are those that allow two way communication between the computer and its operator. In some cases the computer may not be recognisable as a computer. Some examples will amplify this concept.

Microsoft's EasyLiving project aims to develop ubiquitous computer interfaces that can be used in the home or workplace without the user having to sit in front of a workstation. Instead, the user is free to walk around the living space, the computer tracks the user via video cameras installed to monitor the entire space. Having located the user in some room, the system activates microphones, a keyboard and screen in that room, the user may talk to the computer or use the keyboard in that room.

Siemens have developed a GestureComputer and suggested a number of potential applications. The system tracked the users' hands and head and interpreted their motions appropriately. These two examples are simply alternative implementations of the computer keyboard and were intended to improve productivity by easing the communication bottleneck.

MIT developed a substantial application, the SmartRoom, to demonstrate the results of a number of research projects. Among the technologies involved was a module to track people in the room, to interpret their gestures and to provide feedback as appropriate to the task being performed.

A final, slightly trivial example was developed by Mitsubishi. They cited a survey that claimed that the two electronic innovations that most improved American's standard of living were the microwave oven and the television remote control. Mitsubishi set out to improve the remote control. They suggested using a multimedia system to monitor the viewer and interpret suitable hand gestures as control signals for the remote control.

These example systems are still largely in the research stage. However, they do serve to illustrate the fact that multimedia systems provide a richer set of communication channels between the user and the system.

The overall aim of these is to ease the problem of communication with a computer: using a keyboard is an acquired skill, whereas talking or making gestures is, for most people, an everyday occurrence.

What Topics does the Book Cover?

This book does not set out to cover all of the topics listed by the IEEE report quoted above. Instead, it presents the foundations of multimedia delivery systems and an overview of current research into multimedia interactivity.

The following three chapters cover the requirements and implementations of data coding algorithms for sound, images and video data; the methods of assembling multimedia presentations and the hardware platforms required of multimedia systems. These chapters do not set out to teach how to design and build multimedia programmes, rather the intention is to give an overview of the requirements of these systems and directions as to how to assemble the components.

The remaining chapters of the book present an overview of current research in multimedia human-computer interaction: speech understanding, gaze following, gesture recognition and motion following.

Bibliography

Tsuhan Chen (1997) The past, present and future of multimedia signal processing. *IEEE Signal Processing*, 14.
Cipolla R, Pentland A (eds) (1998) *Computer Vision for Human–Machine Interaction*, CUP, Cambridge.
Hodges ME, Sasnett RM (1993) *Multimedia Computing*, Addison–Wesley, Harlow.
Tannenbaum RS, (1998) *Theoretical Foundations of Multimedia*, Computer Science Press.
Vaughan T (1998) *Multimedia: Making It Work*, Osborne.

Part I

2 Perception and Data Coding

Introduction

One of the aims of multimedia delivery systems is to present image or sound data that appears or sounds realistic. That is, the sound quality matches our expectations or the images appear realistic. Obviously the data must be acquired before it can be delivered, and if realistic data is to be delivered, then realistic data must be captured. The subject of Chapter 2 is the capture and storage of realistic data.

As we are aiming to deliver multimedia data that appears to be realistic, the first question to be asked is "what does *realistic* mean?" This must be answered from a study of human perception. If we are able to define the limitations of human perception, then we can set minimum limits to the accuracy with which we should capture data. It will turn out that these limits are, in practice, unattainable with current technology, since humans are able to perceive data to an extremely fine resolution, nevertheless, this study will present standards by which we may judge multimedia delivery systems. These limits will also provide goals for the development of data delivery systems.

The chapter is divided into four sections discussing human perception, capture of data, storage of data, and giving a brief overview of hardware used to capture and replay data.

Perception of Multimedia Data

In an ideal virtual environment, a "client" would experience the full range of sensory inputs. He or she would see the scene in which they were immersed, they would hear the sounds being generated, they would feel objects with which they came into contact, they would smell and taste whatever could be smelt or eaten. The sensory inputs would be indistinguishable from the real world inputs, in fact, the ideal virtual environment could easily be confused with the real world. However, such a virtual environment is some way from being realised, and it is not certain that it is even feasible. In the meantime, virtual environments are almost exclusively restricted to providing sight and sound stimuli.

In developing virtual environments, the human visual and auditory systems are studied to determine the limits of the perception of visual and sound data. Knowing these limits allows the designers to specify the resolution of the data to be presented if the data is to look at all realistic. This section of the chapter will examine how we hear sounds, and how we view images and image sequences. We are addressing questions such as:

1. what range of sounds can be heard?
2. what ranges of colours can be seen?
3. how quickly must discrete images be presented for them to blur into a moving image?

These are the subjects of the following sections looking at the perception of sound, static images and moving images.

Perception of Sound

Sound waves are generated by an object in vibration. The object could be the vocal chords of a speaker, the cone of a loudspeaker in an audio system, or the strings in a piano. The vibrating object alternately compresses and rarefies the air in contact with it. The compressions and rarefactions propagate away from the object, thereby transmitting the sound as a compression wave. Figure 2.1 indicates the magnitude of the pressure changes along the direction that the wave travels. The sound wave has two characteristic properties: its wavelength (measured in metres) or frequency (measured in Hertz, 1 Hz being equal to one cycle per second) and its amplitude. Sound has a constant velocity of approximately 440 ms^{-1} in air, and since the wave's velocity is the product of its frequency and wavelength, knowledge of one implies knowledge of the other. The wavelength or frequency of a sound wave is responsible for its pitch: sound waves of shorter wavelengths or higher frequencies are higher in pitch. The amplitude of the wave is responsible for the sensation of loudness it generates.

If the wave reaches an ear, it may be heard as the ear converts the sound wave's pressure variations into nerve signals that are transmitted on to the brain. A cross section of the human ear is shown in Figure 2.2. Sound waves that reach the ear are directed along the auditory canal and strike the eardrum, setting it in motion. The motion is transferred via the three small bones to the small window of the middle ear and the fluid inside the middle ear is set in motion. The pressure waves within

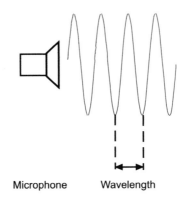

Microphone   Wavelength

Figure 2.1 Generation and propagation of a sound wave

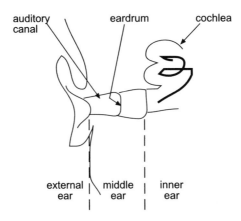

Figure 2.2 Schematic diagram of the cross section through the ear

the fluid are converted into electrical signals by nerve endings in the cochlea and transmitted to the brain. The auditory regions of the brain interpret these electrical signals as the "sounds" that we hear.

The ear detects sounds over a comparatively small range of frequencies, between about 20 Hz and 20 kHz, and is most sensitive in the 2 to 4 kHz range. This is illustrated in Figure 2.3 which shows the relative sensitivity of a typical adult to sounds of the same loudness over the range of audible frequencies. The range of detectable frequencies decreases with age, a child's upper hearing limit may exceed 20 kHz, an elderly person's upper limit may be as low as 10 kHz.

Sound waves seldom have the simple structure suggested by Figure 2.1, in fact this only ever occurs when a simple object, a tuning fork for example, is executing simple harmonic motion. Everyday objects vibrate with complex and unique motions and the sound waves generated by this motion are equally complex and unique. We may decompose the sound generated by a vibrating object into its simple components. This

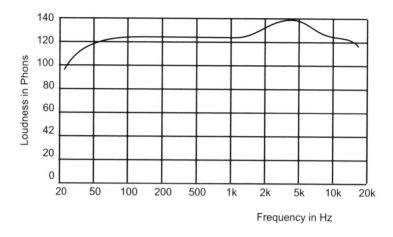

Figure 2.3 Schematic diagram of the typical auditory response at a single sound level

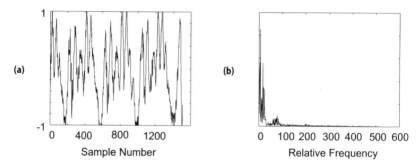

Figure 2.4 (a) a sound signal; (b) the frequency components of the signal

will reveal that most sounds have components spanning most of the range of frequencies we can hear. Figure 2.4 illustrates this, showing how the air pressure, or sound intensity varies with time as the sound "aaaa" is spoken and also the breakdown of this signal into its various frequency components.

Humans are able to detect sounds of an extremely large range of loudnesses. At the quiet end of the scale we would have whispered speech, a library or a quiet recording studio, whilst at the loud end of the scale we would have a nearby pneumatic drill or a jet engine. A sound's loudness is measured by comparison with the quietest sound that can be heard, and is expressed as a decibel (dB). A ratio of 0 dB corresponds to the threshold of hearing, whilst a nearby pneumatic drill could be as loud as 120 dB. Sounds louder than 120 dB can cause pain and hearing loss. It has been suggested that humans are able to distinguish some 350 sound loudness levels.

Perception of Static Image Data

The visual world is perceived because light reflected from surfaces in it is focussed onto light sensitive cells in the eye. These convert the light energy to electrical signals that are transmitted on to the brain and there interpreted as the objects we "see". Figure 2.5 illustrates schematically the gross anatomy of the eye and will be used to describe this mechanism. The eye contains structures whose purposes are first to regulate the amount of light entering it, second to focus rays of light from objects at varying ranges onto the retina and third the retina itself whose major purpose is to encode the image pattern into nerve signals.

Light reflected from a surface in the scene is focussed on the retina in a two stage process. The curved outer surface of the eyeball provides the primary focussing, but the variable focussing that is required to enable us to clearly see objects at different ranges is achieved by changing the refractive power of the eye's lens.

The amount of light entering the eye is regulated partly by the iris. In dark conditions, more light is needed to enable us to see clearly and consequently the iris dilates. The iris contracts in bright conditions so admitting less light. However, the iris diameter changes only by a factor of four, its area therefore changes by a factor of sixteen which is much less than the range of brightness levels over which we can comfortably see. The changing iris size is therefore insufficient to explain the eye's brightness adaptation. In fact, the changing iris size provides a fine control over the eye's adaptation, the major control is achieved by the retina itself changing its sensitivity: in bright conditions, the retina is actually less sensitive to light. This is analogous to the case of a photographic camera, exposure control is achieved by varying the sensitivity of the film and by changing the aperture of the lens.

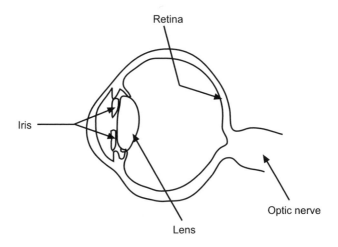

Figure 2.5 Schematic diagram of the cross section through the eye

Anatomical studies reveal that the retina contains some hundreds of millions of light sensitive cells, whilst the optic nerve carries only some hundreds of thousands of individual nerve fibres. A significant amount of data reduction must therefore occur in the retina. It is suggested that the data reduction is achieved by the retina sending difference signals onwards to the brain.

Spatial and temporal differences are computed. Spatial differences are simply the differences in the image data computed between adjacent regions of the same image. Temporal differences are the differences between the same region in temporally adjacent images. The latter effect can be illustrated by staring fixedly at a static scene, without blinking or moving the eyes. Gradually the scene will fade to grey as the temporal differences fall to zero throughout the image. The scene can be regenerated by introducing some movement – either in a component of the scene or by moving the eyes.

When we view a scene, two factors influence the quality of the perceived data: the angular resolution of the eye and the colour/brightness resolution of the eye. These in turn are dictated by the eye's anatomy and physiology: the number and distribution over the retina of light sensitive cells and how these cells react to light of different brightnesses and wavelengths.

The retina contains two types of light sensitive cell, called rods and cones because of their general shape. The rods are generally sensitive to the intensity of light striking them. The cones are further divided into three subtypes according to their sensitivities to light of different wavelengths. The rods and cones are distributed across the retina as shown in Figure 2.6. The colour sensitive cones are highly concentrated at or near to the optic axis and largely absent from the remainder of the retina, a consequence of this is that our peripheral vision is almost monochrome.

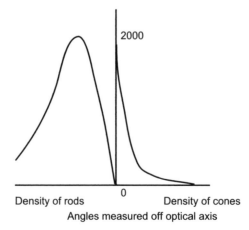

Figure 2.6 Distribution of rods and cones over the retina. The number of rods or cones has been estimated in an area of 0.0069 mm^2

Conversely, the rods are most highly concentrated just off the eye's optical axis and are distributed somewhat more evenly over the entire retinal surface. The rods' distribution has two consequences: our spatial resolution in the peripheral visual regions is very poor, an object must be large or fast moving for us to see it; and since the rods have their highest concentration just off-axis, we can see dimly illuminated objects most clearly by looking at them indirectly.

The maximum concentration of light sensitive cells is in the foveal region on the eye's optic axis. The cells in this region are exclusively colour sensitive cones, there may be approximately 2000 cones in a region that is approximately 100 μm across. The sizes of the cones varies slightly, the smallest are 1 μm across and subtend an angle of 20 seconds of arc. This figure will suggest a size for the smallest discernible object of 0.2 mm at a range of 1 m. In fact our visual acuity is better than this, because we make use of the information from more than a single cone or rod.

Physiological studies have shown that at any one brightness adaptation, approximately 40 shades of brightness may be distinguished. If you were to fixate on a single spot in an image, you would be able to distinguish the 40 shades of brightness. In fact we are able to see significantly more shades within an image because our brightness adaptation continuously alters as we scan over the image.

Our visual system is much more sensitive to colour information. Studies have shown that some 7 500 000 different shades of colour may be discerned. Much effort has been directed towards selecting a minimal set of colours or finding methods of automatically choosing a set of colours that will adequately represent a scene. One resultant scheme (GIF) uses only 256 adaptively selected colours. Other schemes which represent colours by a triplet of red, green and blue values, have no need to select colours, since over 16.7 million colours may be represented by a triplet of eight bit values.

Perception of Moving Image Data

By suggesting that the eye functions in a manner analogous to a still camera, it may be thought that the human visual system functions by capturing and processing discrete versions of the scene being perceived, much as discrete images of a video are captured and processed. However, this is not the case, humans actively interrogate a scene, the phrase "casting one's eye over" describes the process accurately: rather than see and comprehend an entire scene in a single process, the scene is comprehended in a piecemeal fashion. This process takes a finite time, if the scene changes within that time, then some of the changes will not be seen.

When objects in motion are viewed we may focus our attention exclusively on the moving object. We are able to track it smoothly because the image of the object is fixated on the retina; all other components of the scene may be blurred if the object moves sufficiently fast as there will be insufficient time for the observer to "see" the changing background. In a similar manner, if a sequence of images is presented, each image may be fully comprehended if the rate at which they are presented is sufficiently slow. If they are presented at a rapid rate, then the individual images fuse and are not seen as separate images, rather as a "moving" image. For most normal people in a normally lit environment, the critical rate is 20 frames per second. Any sequence of images presented more rapidly than this is seen as smoothly varying data.

Conclusions

We conclude this section by stating that humans are able to hear sounds in the range of 20 to 20 000 Hz and can distinguish some 350 loudness levels. We see with an angular resolution of 20 seconds of arc at best, and can distinguish 40 shades of grey or some 7 500 000 different colour shades. Images presented at a rate higher than about 20 per second fuse and are perceived as moving smoothly.

Capture of Multimedia Data

Having stated the limits of human perception of sound, image and video data, we may now use these quantities to derive lower limits to the resolutions with which these data should be captured, if we are to capture perceptually realistic information. The descriptions that follow will discuss how audio, image and video data is captured and represented in digital form.

In the descriptions, Nyquist's theorem is of fundamental importance. It dictates how a signal should be sampled if the original is to be reconstructed unambiguously from the samples. Briefly, Nyquist demonstrated that a signal must be sampled at twice the frequency of its highest component if reconstruction is to be possible. For example, Figure 2.7 shows a simple harmonic wave; the frequency of the signal is defined by the number of complete oscillations it makes in one second. Nyquist's theorem states that the samples must be taken at a frequency of at least twice this rate: the points indicated on the diagram by solid circles. For a simple harmonic signal having a frequency of 10 kHz, Nyquist's theorem dictates a sampling rate of 20 kHz. If the signal is sampled at a slower rate, corresponding to the open circles, then the original signal cannot be reconstructed, instead the dashed line is reconstructed.

Nyquist's theorem can be stated in three forms, appropriate for sound, image and video capture. For capturing sound, the signal must be sampled at a frequency that is at least twice the highest frequency present

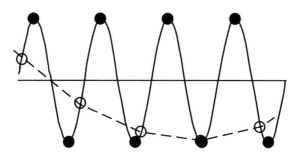

Figure 2.7 Schematic diagram to illustrate the Nyquist frequency

in the signal. For image data, at least two spatial samples must span the smallest dimension of the smallest object that is to be detected. And for video data, there is the additional requirement that two temporal samples must cover the shortest duration event that is to be detected. In all cases, the more samples that are captured, the better will be the quality of the captured data, Nyquist's sampling frequency represents the theoretical minimum. It should also be noted that Nyquist's theorem dictates the lowest resolution for recognising the presence of an object or sound. If the object is to be recognised, then significantly higher sampling rates are required, possibly up to ten to fifteen samples should span the object.

Capturing Sound

Sound data is captured by connecting a sound transducer into a digitiser. The transducer could be a microphone, or any other device that converts the audio energy into a proportional electrical signal. In this signal, a voltage level exactly mirrors the audio data. The signal is captured using an analogue to digital converter (ADC) that samples the signal every nth second, a rate or frequency called the sampling rate or sampling frequency. The sampling resolution, the number of bits assigned to each sample is known as the sample size. It is important to relate the sampling frequency and size to perceptual attributes of the data.

A minimum sampling frequency can be decided using Nyquist's theorem and our knowledge of human hearing. We hear sounds up to a maximum frequency of about 20 kHz. Sampling data at a frequency of twice this rate will unambiguously capture all of the sound that we can potentially hear. In fact, compact disk (CD) quality recordings are made by sampling at 44.1 kHz. Capturing sound of this quality will require large amounts of storage and may in fact be capturing more data than is justified by the contents of the signal. For example, most human speech occupies the frequency range up to about 4 kHz, which would suggest that a sampling frequency of 8 kHz will yield an adequate, though low quality, representation of the speech.

The choice of sampling resolution greatly effects the quality of the captured sound. The more bits that are available for each sample, the better will be the quality of the replayed data. CD quality dictates 16 bits per sample, the only other alternative at present is 8 bits per sample. Figure 2.8 illustrates two problems associated with digital sound (and digital data in general). First is the problem of quantisation, which arises when fewer sampling levels are available than the human ear can distinguish, i.e. we have stated that humans can distinguish 350 sound levels, sound digitised with a resolution less than this will be of discernibly poor quality. Second is the problem of clipping which is due to the finite sampling range and results in distortion of the sampled sound. Both of these problems can be minimised by careful choice of sampling range and resolution, and careful setting of the input signal level, to match the input of the ADC. The sound quality may also be improved by changing the transfer function of the ADC, instead of having a linear transfer function in which the sample value changes in direct proportion to the sound level, we might use a logarithmic function in which the sample values changes in proportion to the logarithm of the input signal.

In its raw format, digitised sound is represented by a stream of numbers – the sample values. Storing data in this format results in large audio files. For example, one minute of stereo CD quality sound (two channels sampled at 44.1 kHz to 16 bit resolution) will require about 10 Mbytes of storage. Compression of the data is therefore required, it will be discussed below.

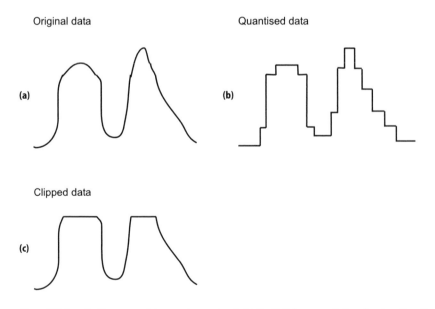

Figure 2.8 Quantisation errors: (a) an analogue signal; (b) its digital representation showing discretisation errors; (c) its digital representation showing clipping, due to overloading of the analogue to digital converter

Capturing Static Image Data

Image data may be captured either by digitising a video signal or by scanning a print of the image. Video capture will be discussed in the following section. Image scanning is today usually achieved by using a flat bed scanner, although a multitude of devices is available. All of the image capture devices will deliver a digital version of the input image.

A digital image is a version of the analogue input that has been digitised in the spatial dimensions and the brightness/colour dimensions (Fig. 2.9), just as the audio signal was sampled at discrete time intervals so the image signal is digitised at discrete spatial intervals, the locations are known as pixels (short for picture elements).

The samples will be equally separated in the two directions, which will yield square pixels and make drawing and processing the data simpler. The magnitude of the separation between samples should be decided by considering the content of the image, the intended use of the data and Nyquist's theorem. As stated above, Nyquist's theorem can be used to infer that two samples must span the smallest dimension of the smallest object that is to be seen in the data. This is a minimal requirement. If we are to recognise the object, a significantly larger number of samples is required. Figure 2.10 illustrates the process. With a small number of samples, objects are detected but cannot be identified. As the number of samples is increased, the identity of the objects becomes clearer.

The input may be sampled as a monochrome image giving pixels whose values are either zero or one. This type of sampling is useful for capturing pages of text for image to text conversion. In capturing the data, the scanner must compute a threshold for each pixel, if the sampled value is above or below the threshold a one or a zero is stored. Methods of computing the threshold have become sophisticated and can give accurate results even for poor quality text.

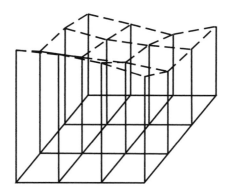

Figure 2.9 Sampling an image. Measurements of the image brightness or colour are taken over a regular grid

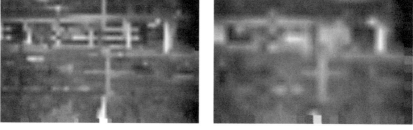

Figure 2.10 The effect of reducing the number of pixels in an image. Smaller objects rapidly disappear, larger ones become unrecognisable. The top right image has 1/4 of the pixels of the top left. Thereafter the number of pixels is reduced by a factor of 4

Alternatively, a grey scale image may be sampled, the pixel values would then reflect the brightness of the input image at that point and would usually be coded as eight bit values, although other options are equally possible. The discussion of human perception suggested that a minimum of about 40 shades of grey is sufficient, more are used to allow some latitude in the capturing process, and to avoid quantisation and clipping errors. Figure 2.11 illustrates these errors by presenting an image with 2, 4, 8, 32, 64 and 256 levels of grey per pixel. Quantisation errors are revealed as false contour lines: where the image suggests a smooth variation in brightness, the poorly digitised data reveals discrete shades

| 8 bits per pixel | 6 bits per pixel |

| 4 bits per pixel | 3 bits per pixel |

| 2 bits per pixel | 1 bit per pixel |

Figure 2.11 The effect of reducing the number of shades of grey in a monochrome image

of grey. Clipping is apparent as areas of saturation, either white or black in regions of very bright or very dark shading.

Finally, the input may be sampled as colour data, in which case three colour component values will be recorded for each pixels: the amount of red, green and blue present at that location. These are usually sampled to the same resolution as the grey scale images. The effects of reducing the number of shades of grey used to represent a pixel may be predicted, smoothly changing regions exhibit contour lines and so on. The effects of reducing the number of colours in a colour image cannot be predicted so easily. The first question to answer is how are the colours represented and therefore how do we reduce the number of colours? Typically, we will observe a remapping of colour values and an increase in the graininess of the image.

The need to encode audio data was demonstrated by simply estimating the storage requirements of a short excerpt of digital sound. The need for coding digital images is much greater. Consider a monochrome image of size 5 inches by 8 inches. Suppose that it is scanned with a spatial resolution of 300 samples per inch (a commonly used resolution) and eight bit values are stored. The captured image will require 3 600 000 bytes. The storage requirements of colour images are tripled as the three colour components are effectively three separate images.

Capturing Video Data

Moving images are most commonly presented as analogue video data. The analogue format is gradually being replaced by digital formats, but analogue video remains the most common format. Many national and international standards exist that specify various video signal formats, in this section we shall describe the standards as they are used in the UK. We shall also discuss how this data may be digitised. Captured video data will have an important part to play when we discuss multimedia interactivity later, since video capture is the method of acquiring data for these systems.

The format of the analogue video signal was specified for the first television broadcasts in the 1930s. Although the details of the specifications have changed, its core remains essentially the same. The video image that we see on the television screen is composed of frames of static data that are presented at a rate of 25 complete frames per second. Each frame is divided into two fields. Although the fields are of lower spatial resolution than the frame, they increase the number of images being presented per second and therefore give the impression of smoother movement. The fields are composed of lines of image data and are arranged such that their lines are interlaced. We therefore see alternate, different, half-resolution versions of the complete video image. The video image can be thought of as a partly discretised image in that it is composed of discrete lines of analogue information.

Today, a television frame is composed of 625 lines of data, divided into two fields of 312.5 lines. The frames update at 25 times per second. The images are drawn on-screen by rectilinearly scanning a point of light whose brightness controls the colour that is drawn on the screen. The point's origin is at the top left of the screen. From there it traces a zig-zag path across and down the screen (Fig. 2.12). Moving across the screen from right to left the point is suppressed, i.e. its brightness is such that it does not draw to the screen. Similarly, as the point retraces from the bottom to the top of the screen it is blanked.

Although the frame is composed of 625 lines of data, not all of this data contributes to the visible image, some lines are deliberately blanked to allow the retracing point to be invisible, other lines contain Ceefax or Teletext information, or quality control information. Some twenty lines are lost. If we wish to digitise the video signal for processing or manipulation, then we can capture at most some 600 lines of data. Many

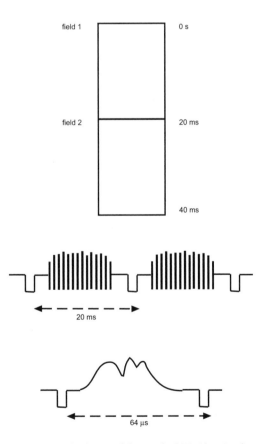

Figure 2.12 The format of the standard UK video signal

commercially available framegrabbers actually capture somewhat less than this number.

The height to width ratio of the video image is 3:4 (it has been suggested that this is the Ancient Greeks' golden ratio that was the most pleasing proportion for a rectangle). This implies that the digitised video image will contain square pixels if we ensure that the number of samples per line is 1.25 times the number of lines in a frame, which evaluates to 780. In practice, some of these points may be discarded as they will lie in the blanked flyback regions of the signal.

If static image data requires a large storage volume, video requires huge volumes. Taking the maximum amount of information from a frame of data, 760 points on 580 lines, storing colour information at three bytes per pixel and capturing the maximum 25 frames per second, 33 Mbytes of storage per second of video data is required.

Coding Multimedia Data

The discussion of the perception of sound and image data has set limits on how much data is required to deliver realistic sound, image or video information. Examples have shown that capturing this data requires a large amount of storage. For example, CD quality sound requires over 10 Mbytes per minute, a moderately sized image can take 3.6 Mbytes, whilst video data will require 33 Mbytes per second. There is a pressing need to compress this data if even small amounts are to be captured and stored.

Two approaches have been taken to coding data, one exploits redundancy by discarding data that is repeated in some way, the other approach discards information that is perceptually insignificant. Redundancy arises in three ways, one or more of which may be present in any signal.

Spatial redundancy arises from the tendency for adjacent samples in the data to have similar values. Our study of visual perception suggested a target data capture rate that was extremely high. This capture rate was dictated by the size of the smallest object being viewed, and will therefore be much too high for most of the image. In this case the probability of adjacent pixels having the same or similar values will be high. Coding schemes may be devised that exploit this. This type of redundancy does not arise in one dimensional sound data.

Spectral redundancy arises from the tendency of equivalent samples from different channels to be similar. For example, in a colour image, the cross-correlations between the red, green and blue values of pixels are high; likewise, the samples derived from a stereo signal are highly correlated. (A high degree of correlation between a pair of signals suggests that their values are co-related: if the value of a sample in one signal is large, then the equivalent sample in the other signal is also likely to be high.)

Finally, temporal redundancy is revealed as samples in a sequence of data resemble each other. For example in an audio signal, the sampling rate will be greater than the rate at which the signal changes, therefore adjacent samples will have similar values, or if we inspected the values of a single pixel in a video sequence, we would observe that those values changed at a slower rate than the rate at which samples are updated. This type of redundancy may be thought of as being a variation on the theme of spatial redundancy. Utilising these data redundancies we shall examine how sound and image data is encoded.

Coding Sound

The necessity for coding sound signals was demonstrated above by considering the volume of storage required for a sampled sound file. The techniques that can be used to code the signal may be tailored for the content of a particular type of signal, or may be general purpose.

The simplest form of coding a sound signal is to simply digitise it, that is to sample and quantise the input waveform. For example, telephone systems band limit signals to the frequency range up to about 3.3 kHz (meaning that any signal of frequency (pitch) greater than 3.3 kHz is not transmitted), the resulting speech is distorted but intelligible. Nyquist's theorem dictates a sampling rate greater that 6.6 kHz, in practice the waveform is sampled at 8 kHz. If a linear quantiser is used (in which the magnitude of the input waveform and the sample are linearly related) then twelve bits per sample are required to yield a signal of acceptable quality. A bit rate of 96 kbits/s results (the bit rate is the rate at which data is captured and must be transmitted or processed). The bit rate may be reduced with no loss of quality by using a suitable non linear quantiser, a logarithmic quantiser is a suitable choice. The sample resolution may be reduced to eight bits, thereby reducing the bit rate to 64 kbit/s, and the reconstructed sound signal is very similar to the original.

Sound sampled at or above the Nyquist frequency will exhibit temporal redundancy. This may be exploited by predictive coding. A predictive coder attempts to predict the following sample using the current one and knowledge of the statistical properties of the sound signal:

$$\hat{s}_t = \alpha\, s_{t-1} + \beta$$

The coefficients α and β are derived by minimising the difference between the predicted value of the sound signal at time t, and the actual value. The coefficients equate to the correlation coefficient and the average value of the signal.

If the predictor is perfect, then the difference between the predicted and actual values will be zero, for all values. In practice, the predictor will be less than accurate and this difference will be finite, but small, certainly much smaller than the original values. It is therefore possible to commit a fewer number of bits to the storage of each error value. Coding schemes that use this method are called differential pulse coded modulation (DPCM) schemes.

The compression may be further improved if the values of the two coefficients are dynamically adapted to the characteristics of the sound signal being coded. Such schemes are termed adaptive differential pulse coded modulations (ADPCM) schemes. International standards were agreed in the 1980s for ADPCM coders that gave bit rates of 32 kbit/s and a reconstructed signal quality very similar to that of the eight bit, logarithmically sampled signals. Later coders operating at 16, 24 and 40 kbit/s were also standardised.

Sound signals may also be coded in the frequency domain. The sound signal may be divided into a number of frequency subbands. Each may be independently coded using an ADPCM coder. The receiver will decode each stream and recombine the signal. Using this scheme it is possible to allocate different resolution values to each subbands coded data. For example, some frequency bands will be perceptually more significant than others. A larger variable is allocated to represent the coded data of these subbands and a smaller variable to the data of perceptually less significant subbands. Such coders attain a better compression rate, but the cost is an increased latency due to the time taken to perform the coding and decoding.

These coding techniques are all suitable for general sound signals. If we wish to define a coder specifically for speech signals, we may obtain higher compression ratios by incorporating more knowledge about the speech generation processes. Chapter 6 will discuss speech generation, for now it is sufficient to state that these coding schemes assume models for the generation and modification of a sound by the human vocal tract. The speech signal is processed to derive values for the parameters of the models. The parameters are transmitted and the receiver performs the decoding using these values. Bitrates as low as 300 bit/s may be achieved, at the cost of a loss of naturalness and occasional loss of intelligibility. These occur because the processes of speech generation are imperfectly understood, the models are therefore approximations to reality.

Coding Still Images

Many individuals and organisations have proposed image coding schemes, but few have gained widespread use. Of these, JPEG is probably the most widely used, perhaps because no commercial restrictions have been placed on its use. This next section will examine the workings of the JPEG image compression scheme, the following section will briefly discuss other schemes.

JPEG

The JPEG image compression standard was drawn up by the Joint Photographic Experts Group (essentially a subcommittee of the International Standards Organisation) and was adopted as an international standard in 1991. Its aim was to derive a method by which continuous-tone, greyscale or colour images could be compressed without loss of visual quality. Since publication the standard has been adopted worldwide as an image compression and storage method.

The JPEG method uses a number of data compression algorithms in sequence, each exploiting data redundancy in a different way. The various parameters required of the algorithms have been set to be optimal for as wide a range of image types as possible. Overall, the algorithms specified by the standard aim to identify the perceptually important information in the image being coded, and discard the unimportant data, compression is therefore achieved at the cost of a loss of information, but the loss should be imperceptible. A schematic diagram of the JPEG architecture is shown in Figure 2.13.

The standard dictates that the image should first be divided into blocks of 8×8 pixels. These are passed through a discrete cosine transform (DCT) whose purpose is to determine the frequency make-up of the data. Low frequency information (slowly changing grey values) will be revealed as high values in the low order transform coefficients. Since most of the image information is low frequency, it will be found that the low order coefficients have much larger values than do the remaining coefficients. In fact a large proportion of the coefficients will be negligibly small.

The DCT generates real-valued outputs, these are transformed into integer values lying in the range 0 to 255. The threshold values that separate the steps of the quantiser should be determined specifically for each image, display and viewing situation. In practice this is too labour intensive and a set of threshold values have been suggested by the JPEG which are adequate for most cases.

The quantised DCT data is then reordered. Rather than represent the data as a two dimensional array having significant values in the low order entries, the data is read in a zig-zag fashion into a one dimensional array in which the significant values are clustered at one end. The data is finally encoded using Huffman coding which achieves additional compression without loss of data.

The method achieves its compression by recognising the information that is important in the perception of the image and discarding the remainder (the quantisation step), and also by organising the image's information content more efficiently (using the DCT and the zig-zag coding).

It has been observed that compressing the input data by a factor of four to five results in no visible loss of quality. Compressing the data by a factor of sixteen results in good quality data which is sufficient for

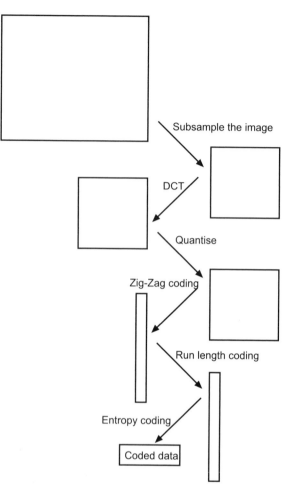

Figure 2.13 A schematic of JPEG image coding algorithm

many applications. Data may be compressed by up to 32× before its quality is degraded to an extent that the data is unusable.

Other Coding Schemes

Despite the ubiquity of the JPEG image coding method, several other schemes are widely used, notably GIF, fractal based techniques and the more recent wavelet based methods.

GIF was proposed as a standard for interchanging graphics data files. It employs an LZW coding scheme that replaces commonly occurring combinations of pixel values with varying length code words. The intention being that the most frequently occurring combination will be represented by the shortest code word and thus achieve compression. The input images are restricted to being eight bits in depth. GIF has suffered recently as the copyright to the LZW algorithm has been enforced, implementers have been required to pay a royalty. Naturally, the JPEG coding techniques are preferable as their use does not involve any payment.

Fractal designs are generated by scaling and placing a simple drawing element according to some rule. With repeated scalings and placements extremely complex scenes can be generated. The technique can be applied in reverse to represent complex scenes with a number of simple primitive elements plus a scaling and placement rule. Although high compression rates and very little loss of quality can be attained, the time taken to compress a single image on moderately powerful hardware is too long to for this method to be widely adopted.

The wavelet transform may be thought of as an alternative to the discrete cosine transform in reordering the information content of an image. Initial studies indicate that it is better than the DCT and replacing the DCT with a wavelet transform could improve the efficiency of the JPEG method.

Coding Video Data

Many propriety video coding methods exist as the organisations that develop video manipulating software define their own. Only one international standard exists, the so-called MPEG standard, in its many incarnations.

MPEG (Moving Pictures Experts Group) is a second committee organised under the International Standards Organisation umbrella. Its activities concern the compression of video and the associated audio data, and the control of their interaction. Since 1989 they have proposed a series of standards dealing with the representation and transport of audio-visual data.

The first standard which became known as MPEG-1 was concerned with the specification of digital video for storage on and reading from CD-ROM. It specified a maximum transmission rate of 1.5 Mbyte/s, which implies a significant compression rate (recalling that full screen video requires a data rate of 33 Mbyte/s for the images alone). MPEG-1 was to deliver VHS quality data (that is, the same quality as is obtained from a domestic video recorder). If the playback of a video tape is frozen, the extremely poor quality of the images will be revealed, but the human visual system is able to interpolate between the poor quality images and derive a reasonably good quality moving image. The coded data was to include the video, audio and control streams, 1.150 Mbyte/s was to be assigned to the video data, 0.256 Mbyte/s to the audio and the remaining 0.094 Mbyte/s to the system.

The compression algorithm was also required to allow random access to the individual frames, to allow fast forward/reverse searches, reverse playback, audio-visual synchronisation, as well as several other minor features.

The solution MPEG proposed included predictive and interpolative coding and relied on a variation of the JPEG coding scheme. The video stream was first divided into three types of frame arranged as shown in Figure 2.14: intraframes, predicted frames and bidirectionally interpolated frames. The intraframes are coded using an algorithm similar to the JPEG scheme. They provide a means of randomly accessing the data, even if there is a limited number of random access points.

In the two prediction schemes that are used, the image is divided into blocks of 16 × 16 pixels. Predicted frames are derived from the previous I- frame using motion compensated prediction. This assumes that blocks do not change their configuration, merely their location. Discovering the motion parameters of individual blocks of data in the pair of I- and P-pictures will allow significant data reduction: the motion parameters alone need be recorded for each block of the P-frame.

B-frames are derived from the closest pair of I- and P-frames. Again motion prediction is used, but rather than look for an exact match between a pair of blocks in an I-frame and the one being coded, the closest match is found between blocks in the previous and following I- and/or P-frame. All of the blocks in the intervening B-frames are then interpolated and the errors between the true and interpolated frames are recorded.

The first MPEG standard was released in 1992, it has since been joined by three others. MPEG-2 (1994) was intended to specify coding techniques for digital television and asynchronous transmission networks. It

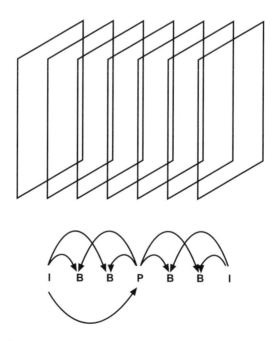

Figure 2.14 A diagram illustrating the relationships between the three types of MPEG frames

therefore had a higher data rate (15 Mbyte/s) which enabled higher quality images and sound to be transmitted. The standard included specifications for incorporating interlaced video (necessary for television signals), for scalable coding (to enable the systems to function when the available bandwidth altered) and for graceful degradation as errors appeared in the data.

MPEG-4 was due for release at the end of 1999. Rather that be concerned with how digital video and television should be represented and transmitted, this standard takes a somewhat more abstract viewpoint and is concerned with how multimedia objects ought to be coded, and how their interactions can be specified. The user is able interact more fully with the data, rather than simply stop and start the sequence.

Coding/Decoding Hardware

Coding and decoding of data is a computationally intensive process. Historically, when processors were of limited power, it was necessary to add additional task-specific hardware to perform data compression or decompression within tolerable time limits. With the processing power available to today's processors, most of these tasks can be performed by the processor itself. The one exception to this is the generation of sound data.

All desktop computers have had the capability of playing sound via a built in speaker. The quality of this sound has been poor as the speaker is small and low powered; the volume, dynamic range and frequency response have all been poor. This state was greatly improved by the introduction of the sound card, an add-on device that was designed to drive high powered speakers. Most sound cards also have the hardware necessary to capture sound data.

Displaying multimedia data on a desktop computer does not generate a realistic experience. We are immersed in the world and therefore receive stimuli from all directions, a desktop system can deliver sound from all directions, but is limited in the amount of visual data it can present. Alternative systems must be used to create truly immersive environments. Some systems require a user to wear a head mounted display, a pair of small video screens is used to display what the user would see in his virtual world. As the user moves his head, the system recomputes the user's views – such systems are easy to use but require large amounts of computation to update the image data, and are limited to one user at a time. Other systems create the immersive environment by using large video projection walls – the virtual world data is projected onto a cubic space made up of these walls, the users sit or stand inside the cube. The hardware required to set up a system is expensive, but the computational throughput is less and the environment can be used by many users at a time.

Conclusions

This chapter has examined the methods of capturing digital audio, images and video, deriving the capture requirements from a study of human perception. The volumes of storage required by the captured data dictate that compression algorithms are used. These have also been examined.

Bibliography

Printed Material

Day RH (1969) *Human Perception*, John Wiley.
Gall DL (1991) MPEG: a video compression standard for multimedia applications, *Comm ACM*, 34.
Gregory RL (1998) *Eye and Brain*, OUP, Oxford.
Marr D, Vision. WH Freeman and Co, San Francisco.
Wallace GK (1991) "The JPEG Still Picture Compression Standard", *Comm ACM*, 34.
Vaughan T (1998) *Multimedia: Making It Work*, Osborne,

Internet Resources

The Official MPEG website: http://drogo.cselt.stet.it/mpeg/
The unofficial MPEG website: http://www.mpeg.org
What is VR? http://www.cms.dmu.ac.uk/~cph/VR/whatisvr.html
This link contains descriptions of the major types of VR environments, plus links to other sources of information.

3 Organising and Delivering Multimedia Objects

Introduction

The previous chapter examined the requirements for and methods of representing multimedia data types. Coding methods were described, these are required if multimedia data is to be stored and presented to a consumer, since the captured data is extremely voluminous. Human perception was also studied, as the limits of our abilities to see and hear data suggest minimum requirements for presenting realistic appearing data – should realistic data be required. In this chapter, the methods of integrating multimedia components into a coherent presentation are examined. As a starting point we shall assume that the components of the presentation (the text, images, graphical objects, video clips and sounds) have been captured and prepared – Chapter 3 will examine methods of organising their delivery.

The fact that a multimedia presentation is created by the *integration* of diverse data types must be emphasised. A presentation must be more than simply the addition of more types of data to the basic presentation material. Each new component must make a positive contribution to the whole presentation, and must not detract in any way from any other component's contribution.

In this chapter we shall first examine what is required by the consumer of a multimedia presentation. What types of data may be presented, and what methods are there of being presenting with the data? The features required of presentation design tools are examined, with the aim of identifying features that will facilitate the design and implementation of the types of presentation that have been identified. Some of the available tools will be described and evaluated with regard to these requirements.

An alternative method of designing a multimedia presentation, is to implement it as a set of web-pages that may be viewed using any of the freely available browsers. The advantages and disadvantages of this approach will be discussed, and methods of realising the four categories of presentation will be described.

It will become apparent that many design effects may be achieved using the methods described in Chapter 3. But, the ability to achieve a particular effect does not imply that the effect is desirable. The chapter will therefore conclude with an outline of some good design practices. This section is not intended to be exhaustive, rather an overview of generally accepted design principles. This is an area in which it is impossible to set rules, since an effect that is acceptable in one context, or at one time may be anathema in another context or at a different time.

A Classification of Multimedia Presentations

Multimedia presentations may be categorised as in Figure 3.1, according to the degree of freedom that is provided for the consumer to navigate his or her way through the presentation. Four categories of presentation have been identified, ranging from freely navigable ones to presentations in which one piece of information follows another outside of the consumers control.

All presentations are centred around a screen and the information that can be displayed or accessed using that screen. As a simple example, the title sequence of a television programme may be considered to be a presentation; the information being conveyed concerns the programme: its title, its authors, the producers and actors. Each screen conveys a certain amount of information, we may have a title screen followed by a number of screens identifying the participants. The whole presentation is decomposed into a sequence of screens, each of which contains information, in this case some simple text.

Browsing

This category of presentation is an extreme and is seldom found in practice as it is both difficult to create and hard to convey any coherent

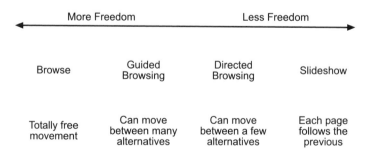

Figure 3.1 A categorisation of Multimedia Presentations

message using it. But, given a small number of screens of information such a presentation may be created. Its defining characteristic is the ability to access any screen of the presentation from any other screen, Figure 3.2. Clearly, it is this characteristic that makes this type of presentation unwieldy, since the number of connections that must be made from one screen increases in proportion to the number of screens. Whilst this is technically feasible, it is undesirable from a presentation viewpoint as the consumer will rapidly lose track of which screens have been visited and what information was presented there. It is fundamentally a disorganised scheme.

Guided Browsing

Guided browsing implies a more organised presentation as the user's choice of which screens of a presentation to view are context dependent. That is, a small choice of destinations is available at any one page, as suggested in Figure 3.3. This is the model of presentation that is typically used in most internet sites, the screens may be organised hierarchically and a small number of sub-screens made accessible from a screens at a given level. This model provides the advantage that the information being presented on a screen and its sub-screens may be conceptually related, and the user's path through them is therefore much simpler.

Directed Browsing

Directed browsing is a special case of guided browsing in which there is exactly one link between one screen and the next in a presentation. The user is able to consume the information present on a screen before

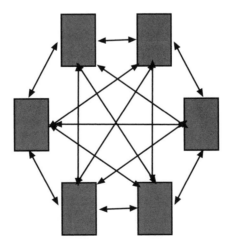

Figure 3.2 A browsing presentation

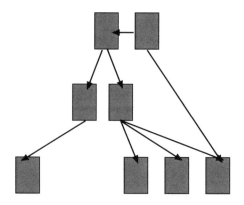

Figure 3.3 A guided presentation

deciding to move to the following one. A typical example may again be drawn from the presentation of some academic papers on the Internet in which the paper is divided into a number of web-pages according to its division into sections, the reader is allowed to move from one section to the following one.

Slide Presentation

The slide presentation is a further specialisation. It conceptually follows the model of the directed browsing presentation, but the consumer has no control over when the presentation advances between screens. The example of the television title sequence has already been cited. Although it may seem to be a simple and restrictive model with little applicability, it has found its niche for presentations that are to be made continuously without intervention, Figure 3.4 illustrates the pages' organisation.

Review

This section has reviewed four classifications of multimedia presentation. They share common characteristics: each presentation is decomposed into screens (also known as pages) that should be conceptually self contained, Figure 3.5. The presentation provides links between pairs of screens, one or more links may appear per screen, and the links may be activated by the consumer or automatically by the presentation itself after

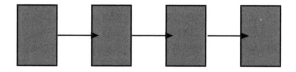

Figure 3.4 A directed presentation and a slide presentation

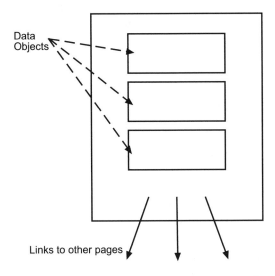

Data Objects

Links to other pages

Figure 3.5 The characteristics of a screen (page) in a presentation

a predetermined time delay. Most design tools allow the designer to associate apparently sophisticated effects with the changing of the page.

Multiple data types may be presented from within each screen – their presentation may be automatic or under the consumer's control. At the very least there will be a single data object on a screen. The designer of the presentation must decide the material to be presented, the order of the presentation and the mechanism by which the presentation will occur. Design tools are available to assist with this task, but, as with all tools, they will not perform the task automatically.

What is Required of a Multimedia Presentation Design Tool?

A multimedia presentation design tool will aid in the design of a multimedia presentation. It will not create the raw materials of the presentation and it will not organise the presentation. These are tasks that the designer must do, and no self-respecting designer would want them to be automated. Having created the components of the presentation and decided how they will be presented, the design tool must provide the designer with the facility to incorporate the components into the finalised presentation also the facility to organise how and when the components are to be displayed. The term "authoring system" has been coined to describe a tool such as this.

A presentation design tool must aid the designer in realising his design. It must aid in the placing of components, especially when one component overlies another. The tool must allow the designer to control the timings of components' appearances and disappearances, and the transitions between pages, if this is to be performed automatically. Finally, the tool must allow the designer to control any user interactivity, it must error check any input and respond as appropriate. Several models of authoring system have been implemented, they are the subject of the following section.

Characteristics of Practical Design Tools

Four major models have been suggested for describing the design methods implemented in the wide range of available authoring tools. They differ according to the metaphor used for representing the sequence of events that will occur in the presentation. Some are tools in which each stage of the presentation is represented as a card or a screen; others organise events along a timeline, the events are thus tied to a specific time in a sequential organisation. Other tools represent multimedia activities as nodes (which could represent multimedia objects or events) in a directed graph structure and are described as icon based tools. Finally there are object oriented tools in which the components and events are considered as objects that are hierarchically related.

Card Based Tools

Card based tools represent the screens of the presentation as pages of a book, or the cards of an index file. The tool will allow links to be made between the individual cards which will result in the consumer of the presentation being able to navigate between linked cards. Multimedia elements must be attached to the card from which they are to be launched, for example, an animation may be required on a particular card. Apple's HyperCard is a popular example. Underlying the graphical editor for the creation and linking of cards will be scripting language. The graphical design will be converted into a "programme" in the scripting language, which will be interpreted at run time.

Timeline Based Tools

In this metaphor, the multimedia presentation is represented as a musical score. The different parts of the score represent the different components of the presentation. The score orchestrates each component, indicating its lifetime and ensuring cross component synchronisation. Macromedia's Director uses this model. The timeline may be very finely divided, its resolution could be as small as one television frame.

Icon Based Tools

These tools represent the components and the interaction cues of a presentation as icons that are interconnect along a flow line according to the sequence of actions that are planned to occur. The tools allow rapid development of presentations but are not the speediest in execution. Nevertheless, they remain very popular.

Object Oriented Tools

Multimedia elements and events become objects that exist in a hierarchical structure. A message passing protocol is used to instruct an object to perform some action. The objects themselves are programmed to perform some action in response to some message. For example, a video object may have an associated "play" action, as could a sound object. The two objects would respond very differently to a message instructing them to "play". One advantage of the methodology is that the objects become self contained and abstracted away from their user, once a video object is created, that inherits generic video properties, the designer need not be concerned with how the object and its methods are implemented, rather he may concentrate on their use.

Implementing Multimedia Presentations Using HTML

Possibly the simplest method of implementing a multimedia presentation is to use a simple word processor and create the presentation as a set of hypertext markup language (HTML) documents to be viewed using a standard web browser, such as Netscape or Internet Explorer. The syntax of the markup language is summarised in Appendix 1, this section of Chapter 3 will outline and illustrate some of its uses.

An HTML document is a piece of text into which markup tags have been embedded. The tags are interpreted by a browser as commands to control the formatting of the text or other multimedia components and the document links that might be followed. The remaining text is drawn to the screen. Tags are indicated by angle brackets.

The start and end of an HTML document should be indicated by the start and end of HTML tags. Within these tags, the document should be divided into its head and body. The head of the document will contain instructions concerning the appearance of the document's window in the browser, the body will contain additional tags plus the information to be presented, Figure 3.6.

Within the head of the document the body tag is used to specify the appearance of the document. A background image may be specified with its uniform resource locator (URL). The document's background colour

```
<HTML>
<HEAD>
<TITLE> any text </TITLE>
</HEAD>
body of page
</BODY>
</HTML>
```

Figure 3.6 The syntax of the simple HTML document

may be changed from the default grey. The text's colour may be changed from its default and the colours taken by hyperlinks, active hyperlinks and visited hyperlinks may also be changed. Figure 3.7 describes the syntax. In this syntax, colours are specified by six digit hexadecimal values. The digits are taken in pairs, the first pair indicates the red contribution to the resulting colour, the other two represent the amounts of green and blue.

One of the most used properties of a web page is its ability to link in other hypertext documents (without this property the Internet would not exist as it does and would certainly not be as well used as it is). The links are specified using anchors, whose syntax is shown in Figure 3.8. The anchor tag starts with a URL to another document and ends with the end anchor tag. Between these two is the object that will appear as the link in the webpage. Normally, this would be a piece of meaningful text, but it could also be a graphical object.

The final HTML component to be considered is the list. These will be encountered very rapidly when web pages are viewed. The syntax of the tags used to express a list is shown in Figure 3.9. Two variants of the list exist – ordered and unordered lists. Using the first results in a sequence of numbered listed items. The second results in a bulleted list of items. Lists may be embedded inside other lists. The items to be listed could be any object, lists of URLs seem to be most common.

```
<BODY BACKGROUND = 'url'
BGCOLOR = #dddddd
TEXT = #dddddd
LINK = #dddddd
VLINK = #dddddd
ALINK = #dddddd>
```

Figure 3.7 The BODY tag

```
<A HREF = "url">linkname</A>
```

```
<A HREF = "week1\index.html">online</A>
   the lecture slides are available online
```

Figure 3.8 The ANCHOR tags

```
<UL>
<LI> item 1              ● item 1
<LI> item 2              ● item 2
</UL>
```

Figure 3.9 The syntax of the list tags

Good Design Practice

Style is very much a personal and evolving issue; what is appealing to one person at one time may be revolting to another, or even the first person at a different time! However, it is possible to state certain rules of style that should be adhered to as they affect the intelligibility of a multimedia presentation

All presentations should have a structure and a purpose. The comprehensibility of a presentation is enhanced if its structure is readily inferred. The structure need not be made explicit, but it should exist. How the material of a presentation is to be organised should be apparent once the purpose of the presentation has been determined. A presentation should have a purpose that is self evident, such a presentation can only be improved if its intended purpose is adhered to and no side-tracking is allowed.

All presentations must be given a title, the authors' names should be published, as should any acknowledgements. In addition, if the presentation is to be published on the Internet, it should be given a status (is this a final document, a first draft, or rambling thoughts?) and a date to indicate its currency; some method of providing feedback to the document's author is often helpful.

Multimedia presentations will be viewed on a range of hardware platforms. The primary differences between platforms will be varying screen resolutions and processor speeds, which will change how a presentation behaves. It is therefore sensible to test a presentation on a range of platforms and include only those elements that make positive contributions to the presentation and are not degraded by being viewed on a less powerful platform. This requirement also has the advantage of preventing media overload – in which a multitude of components have been included in a presentation simply because they could be incorporated.

Manipulating Multimedia Content

A multimedia presentation may contain textural elements, images and graphical elements, video clips and sound clips. The raw data can be captured using the devices described in other chapters. However, the data is seldom captured in a form that is suitable for the final presentation, image data may have become corrupted by noise, the colour balance of an image may be incorrect, and so on.

Capturing Data

The different types of component of a multimedia presentation must be captured using different techniques. Text will be "captured" using some form of wordprocessor. The wordprocessor need not have any sophisticated features since the text will probably be manipulated further. Audio data will probably be captured using the recording equipment built in to the soundcard of the PC.

Images may be captured using a scanner, or possibly by downloading directly from a digital still camera. Artwork can be developed using any drawing package, paying attention to the format of the saved files and their resolutions, as discussed below.

Video data can be captured in one of three ways. A dedicated video capture card may be added to the computer. This will be able to capture analogue video and store it to disk in real time. The image quality will be high. The capture cards are expensive, their price is similar to that of the computer itself. Alternatively, video capture may be performed using the host computer's graphics system. This will sometimes require additional hardware that is piggy-backed onto the graphics card. The captured data will not be of such high quality as that captured by a dedicated card, but it will be satisfactory for most purposes. Finally, with the advent of digital video cameras comes the possibility of interfacing the camera directly to the computer and downloading digital video. Networking standards have been agreed (e.g. Firewire) for interfacing suitably equipped devices, video cameras were amongst the first of these.

Editing Data

However much care has been taken when capturing data, errors may be introduced. For example, the captured sound may contain unwanted silences, or the colour balance of an image may be incorrect. The designer of the presentation might also want to alter the data before including it in the presentation. This section will briefly discuss errors that can be introduced in to the data, the effects that might be required, and the requirements of data manipulation tools.

Text Editing Tools

The author of any text has the responsibility of ensuring that the text is correct, that is, it contains no factual, spelling nor grammatical errors. It is the presentation designer's responsibility to determine how the text should be presented, that is, its layout on the screen or page, its size, font and colour. Most modern word-processing or desktop publishing tools can be used to accomplish this.

Sound Editing Tools

Typical errors that are found in sound segments include unwanted silences, unbalanced stereo recordings or an incorrect spectral balance. Any sound manipulation programme should have the capability of allowing a user to modify the data to correct these errors. The programme should also be able to add in special effects as they are required.

Perhaps the most important function of a sound editing tool is to change the resolution of the stored data. Whilst any sound clip should be recorded to the best possible resolution (i.e. highest sampling rate and largest number of bits per sample), this data is generally not appropriate for distribution. The sound editing tool must therefore be able to write the data in other formats. The presentation designer will have carefully specified the format of the sound with regard to the required quality and the intended delivery platform.

Image Editing Tools

Digitised images can suffer from a number of degradations introduced by the capturing process. It is important to note that manipulating a digital image will degrade the quality of the data, thus correcting the errors in a faulty image can result in a perceptually worse image. Images are therefore captured with a resolution that is much higher than the resolution of the image that is included in the final presentation.

Typical errors that might be encountered include framing, orientation and colour balance errors. Framing errors arise when superfluous data has been captured, they may be removed by cropping the image. The contents of the image may also be altered to improve its aesthetics, but this should be done with caution. Orientation errors occur if a scanned image was not oriented correctly during scanning. Whilst it is possible to rotate the image to correct this error, better results would be obtained by rescanning the image.

Colour balance errors can be caused by the scanning process or by the original image capture. Any image editing tool should be able to correct the contrast and brightness of the image as a whole; the hue, saturation and value of the whole image, or be able to manipulate the individual colour planes. The image editing tool should also be able to support simple image manipulation tasks, such as modifying the colours of individual pixels or small regions. This might be necessary to remove red-eye in a portrait, or perhaps to move objects in the image.

Special effects might be added to the image, to enhance its presentation. For example, the border might be blurred, or particular colourising techniques might be applied. It is often tempting to apply these techniques, simply because the image manipulation tool supports these effects. This is a temptation that should be resisted, as uncontrolled application of many special effects can detract from the content of a presentation.

The final, major task of any image manipulation tool is to prepare the image for inclusion in the final presentation. The designer will be aware of the size of the image in the presentation, he will therefore resize the image and possibly alter its colour resolution – displaying an image with a larger colour depth than the platform supports is not recommended.

Video Editing Tools

The errors found in video segments are, surprisingly, similar to those found elsewhere. The recording may not have been correctly framed, the colour balance may be incorrect or the content may need to be manipulated. However, even a moderately short video clip will contain a large number of frames, manipulating all of them may not be an efficient use of time, it may be preferable to recapture the clip avoiding those errors. One exception to this is resizing the video clip, video editing software will allow the user to specify a range of frames to be saved, and the resolution of the saved clip. The software will also allow the editor to splice clips, controlling the fading process.

A major use of video editing software is to reduce the resolution of the data such that the final version is of the correct size for the presentation and the platform that will be used to deliver the presentation.

Format of the Stored Data

Many formats exist for storing the various data types. Some formats are application specific, for example a file created using a particular word-processor is often only readable by that wordprocessor. Other formats are international standards, such as the JPEG image format discussed in the previous chapter. There is also the option of storing the raw data without any format information, but this is not recommended as it can be impossible to subsequently decode the data.

In the past, the "standard" formats were also platform dependent, fortunately this is becoming less of a problem as software developers migrate applications across platforms. For example, video clips used to be stored as QuickTime files on the Macintosh platform and as AVI files on the PC, as it was not possible to play one clip on the other platform – today, this is not the case.

Wherever possible, data should be stored using a widely used format that is appropriate for the data. Sound clips ought to be stored as WAV or MP3 files depending on their content. Images should be stored as GIF or JPEG files, paying attention to the resolution. If an image is displayed at a lower resolution than it was drawn at, then information will be lost – the small details will not be displayed and what were continuous lines may become broken up. Similarly, an image will be seriously degraded if the display supports a smaller range of colours than are present in the image. In this case, the designer should have considered reducing the colour resolution of the image or even converting it to a monochrome version.

The case for digital video formats is not so clear. International standards have been agreed and are used in the broadcasting of video data and in the electronic storage. However, files stored using this format, although compressed, are still very large. Alternative formats have therefore been developed and deployed by the major manufacturers. This is not necessarily a problem, as the formats are supported across all platforms.

Instant Multimedia

This chapter has been concerned with the tools required to implement multimedia presentations. The tools used to capture and prepare the presentation's components and to organise them into coherent presentation have been examined. A presentation could also be implemented using many of the standard office tools. For example, Microsoft Word allows images, sound clips and video clips of various formats to be embedded into a document. It is therefore possible to develop a multimedia presentation using Word and to deploy it as a Word document – other programmes have similar capabilities.

Conclusion

Chapter 3 has examined methods of implementing multimedia presentations, given that the required components have been assembled. A design tool must provide the designer with the functionality to control the timing of the appearances of the presentation's components and must provide methods of controlling how the presentation is to be navigated: is the consumer free to browse the presentation, or does the presentation proceed through a fixed sequence of events?

Many design tools exist. A free alternative to purchasing one is to make use of the hypertext markup language and develop presentations that will be viewed using an Internet browser. Whilst this has cost advantages, the methods involves significantly more work on the designer's part, and the presentations will have significant limitations. Within these limitations however, high quality presentation material may be produced. It can also be argued that this production method is the most prolific, given the high number of Internet users worldwide.

Some of the syntax of HTML was introduced, more is presented in Appendix 1. The language is much more extensive than this description has indicated. Many books are published describing the language and its use. An effective method of learning to use HTML is to experiment with a simple wordprocessor and an Internet browser.

Chapter 3 closed with an overview of some simple design rules. While it is *impossible* to dictate style rules, it is *possible* to make suggestions as to good and bad style elements.

Bibliography

Printed Material

Raggett D, Lam J, Alexander I, Kmiec M (1998) *Raggett on HTML 4.0*, Addison–Wesley, Harlow.
Vaughan T (1998) *Multimedia: Making It Work*, Osborne, Berkeley.

Internet Resources

Many vendors of authoring tools have evaluation copies available for download. Naturally, these versions of the tools are either not fully functional or have a limited lifetime.

Apple: www.apple.com
Adobe: www.adobe.com
Macromedia: www.macromedia.com
Other sites can be found in the comp.multimedia newsgroup's FAQ.
Tim Berners-Lee's good design practice: http://www.w3.org/Provider/Style/All.html

4 Hardware to Support Multimedia Systems

Introduction

A multimedia presentation has been designed and implemented using one of the authoring systems described previously. How can it be viewed – what hardware is required to support the viewing?

The presentation, like any computer programme, may be realised in an executable or interpreted form. In the executable form, the presentation is translated into a format that is directly executable on the computer. The resulting code is then treated simply as any other programme. The interpreted presentation uses a player that will translate the instructions of the presentation into machine executable codes on the fly. An executable presentation will probably require less memory that the presentation plus player combination, it may also execute more quickly than the interpreted presentation.

It is common to have both alternatives available from an authoring tool. The tool may allow the author to save his presentation as a stand-alone package. The viewer would then "execute" this (if the term "execute" is applicable to a task that could be as simple as displaying a piece of text). The authoring tool may also have a freely distributable player for its presentations. The viewer would use the player to view the presentation. As an example of this arrangement, Adobe markets a publishing programme, Acrobat, that enables authors to save document layout files in a specific format. Adobe freely distributes a player that can be used to read and print, but not create files of this format.

In summary, a presentation can normally be delivered as an executable file or as one that must be interpreted by a separate player. Using either option results in some software that is to be executed on some hardware. The design effort will have been wasted if the platform used for the presentation is incorrectly specified: the images may not appear with their correct colours or spatial resolutions, or the video or sound clips will not be played smoothly and may lack synchronisation.

Earlier chapters have discussed the requirements for representing the types of data objects that a multimedia system will present, and the requirements of the software tools that will aid the designer in assembling a presentation. In Chapter 4, we shall examine the hardware needed to support the creation and delivery of multimedia presentations.

The Multimedia PC

What hardware is needed to support the creation and delivery of a multimedia presentation?

This is a question that should perhaps be answered when considering the implementation of multimedia presentations. However we could argue that the hardware required to implement and present the presentation can be very different. The author of a presentation may tolerate inferior performance in his hardware, whereas, if the presentation is to be sold, the customer must be satisfied with the presentation, implying that the content and the delivery must be satisfactory. As a simple example, images may be edited (albeit with a great deal of extra effort) using a monitor that is unable to display the complete image, a customer would be dissatisfied with this level of performance.

When considering a multimedia delivery platform, two alternatives present themselves: the Macintosh and the Multimedia Personal Computer.

From the outset, the Macintosh range of computers has been capable of capturing and presenting multimedia data. When the first Macintosh was presented, the quality of the replayed data was poor by the standards we have come to expect of today's systems. But the data quality has improved as the speed and capacity of the hardware has improved, without requiring changes to the specification of the processor or other components. More importantly, older software can still be executed on the newer machines.

The IBM Personal Computer was intended as a desktop equivalent of a mainframe computer (not necessarily with the same performance characteristics!). There was initially no requirement that the PC be able to manipulate multimedia data.

The multimedia personal computer (MPC) standard was first published in 1990. It described the minimum specification for a multimedia capable personal computer. The level one MPC should contain a 386SX processor, running at a frequency of 16 MHz, it should have 2 megabytes of random access memory and a hard disk with a capacity of 30 megabytes. The screen's dimensions should be a specified number of pixels (VGA resolution) and the MPC should be capable of playing sound digitised to a resolution of eight bits. By today's standards the level one MPC was very primitive, its specification was dictated by what the technology of the day could achieve rather than by the quality we would like in a multimedia presentation.

The standard was upgraded in 1993, but only in response to improvements in the available technology. The processor was updated to a 486SX, the clock speed was increased to 25 MHz, the amount of memory was doubled, the hard disk capacity was increased to 160 megabytes and the audio resolution was doubled. A compact disk (CD) player was also specified. Again, this standard was dictated by the technology, not the requirements of multimedia.

The final specification of the MPC was published in 1995, it specified the MPC according to its abilities, rather than its components. It was a simplification of the original standards as a response to the variations in the specifications of basic PCs. The level three MPC must be able to play video data stored in the MPEG-1 format.

Today, it would be unusual to find a computer that was not described as a multimedia computer. All personal computers sold today are able to play MPEG video with ease. The current aim in the development of the MPC is to exceed the level three requirements by improving the quality of the video image that can be played and improving the computer's interactivity.

Peripheral Devices

The MPC level three standard states that a computer is a multimedia computer if it can play a particular type of multimedia file. In this section, we will consider the hardware that enables this and also discuss the hardware used in multimedia computing generally.

Processor

The heart of any multimedia computer is its processor. Satisfactory presentations may be delivered using an older, lower performance processor, as specified for the MPC. However, the quality of presentation that may potentially be achieved, in terms of the quality of its constituent components, the sophistication of any effects used and the number of simultaneously active components it may support, can only be maximised by using as fast and efficient a processor as available. A useful guide when purchasing a multimedia computer would be to buy the one with the highest specification, realising that the specification will be exceeded in a much cheaper computer within a short period of time.

Storage Media

It has been seen in earlier chapters, that multimedia objects, even though they may be compressed, require large volumes of storage. For example, a five second video clip can be compressed to approximately 400 kilobytes (of poor resolution images). For any storage medium, the general rule to be applied is to have as much as possible.

Random Access Memory (RAM)

Random access memory is volatile storage used to store a programme and the data it is manipulating. The amount of memory supplied with a new computer is large in comparison with the amount supplied in the recent past. However, software is rapidly becoming more sophisticated, and modern software requires these large volumes of memory. Minimum memory requirements increase very quickly; books written only two or three years ago suggested that "MPC3 standard computers required 8 megabytes of memory, but 16 is better and 20 may be required".

The more memory that is available to a computer, the faster a programme will execute. A typical new computer would be supplied with 32 megabytes or more of RAM. The amount of memory available may be increased by using virtual memory – an area of the computer's hard disk that is set aside to act as RAM. In principle the amount of RAM available to a computer could be increased indefinitely, however, accessing data on the hard disk is slower than accessing the real memory and there will be a limit to the amount of disk space that is available.

Disk Drives

There are several types of disk drives, characterised according to whether they are fixed inside the computer or not and their capacity. As with memory, the general rule to be applied when specifying a computer, is to request more than would be immediately required. As with RAM, last year's requirements are generally too small for today's needs.

Hard Disks

The hard disk drive will be fixed inside the computer and is used for long term, non-volatile storage. It has the capacity to store a few gigabytes of data (one gigabyte is a thousand megabytes). Storage capacities are increasing rapidly, two years ago a 2 gigabyte disk was thought to be enormous, at present 10 to 15 gigabytes is a large drive. Whilst the capacities of disk drives are increasing rapidly, so too are the storage requirements of applications. Earlier editions of most packages were always smaller than the later versions, partly due to the increase of features offered by the newer versions (the cynical would also say that software developers no longer code as carefully, knowing that typical users will have disks with large capacities!).

Floppy Disks
Floppy disks provide an excellent means of transferring limited amounts of data between computers or of archiving limited amounts of data. They are of limited use as their capacity is a mere 1.44 megabytes, which is sufficient for perhaps ten JPEG coded images of moderate to good quality and size. Despite this, floppy disks remain a popular means of storing and transferring data.

CD-ROM
Compact disks provide a means of permanently storing larger amounts of data than is possible using a floppy disk. A CD may be written once only but the data is then virtually indestructible. One CD has a capacity of some 760 megabytes. When the first CD-ROM was released, it was able to transfer data at a rate of 150 kilobytes per second (hence the coding limit for MPEG-1 video), which is a rather slow rate. Successive generations of CD-ROMs have had increased transfer rates, hence their specifications mention readers of 12×, 24× or higher.

Zip Drives
Zip drives can be thought of as a high capacity floppy disk. Current versions have a capacity of 100 megabytes, similar components are available having even higher capacity. Apart from the difference in capacity, Zip drives behave in the same manner as the lower capacity floppy disks.

DVD
The Digital Versatile Disk was suggested in 1995 by a consortium of nine major electronics companies to distribute multimedia information and feature length films on disk. Their capacity is higher than CD-ROM, about 4.7 gigabytes, their readout rate corresponds to that required to view full motion video plus high quality sound: about 4.69 megabits/s. Physically, a DVD has the same size and shape as a Compact Disk, but data is written onto the disk at a higher density.

Input Devices

A range of input devices are used in multimedia systems, ranging from the commonplace keyboard and mouse to the esoteric such as the trackball, joystick and touchscreen. This description starts by examining keyboards and pointing devices, then discusses other input devices.

Keyboard

The keyboard is probably the input device most familiar to the widest range of users as it has been used for the longest time for alphanumeric input to a computer. Some systems may require a ruggedised keyboard, if for example it is to be used in a hazardous environment. In this case, the keys would be protected by a plastic membrane to prevent the ingress of liquid or any damaging gases.

Pointing Devices

Pointing devices are used to move a cursor around on screen. They are necessary for the modern wimp interface style (windows, icons, mouse, pointer). In essence, all pointing devices will move a cursor on the screen in response to the user moving the device. It is important that the two movements are proportional, that is, the on-screen cursor moves at a rate and over a distance that are proportional to the rate and amount of movement input by the device.

Mouse
A mouse is a device that translates hand movements over a surface into movement of an on-screen cursor. The mouse will also include one or more buttons whose clicks will be transmitted to the host computer and interpreted according to the software being executed. The mouse may be connected to the computer by wire or by an infra-red link.

Under the mouse is a small ball which is kept in contact with the surface and rolls as the mouse is moved. Two rollers in contact with the ball are connected to optical encoders, or similar devices, that record the movement of the mouse in the forwards and sideways directions. These movements are converted directly into movement of the cursor, the magnitude of the cursor's movement is directly proportional to the magnitude of the mouse movement.

Trackball
A trackball is conceptually the same as a mouse in that the user's movements are translated into cursor movements and button clicks are made possible. The difference is that the unit is stationary, the user moves a ball on top of it to control the cursor. For some users this arrangement enables more accurate control of the cursor position.

Joystick
A joystick provides a lever to control movement of the cursor. The direction in which the level is pushed controls the direction in which the cursor moves. The major difference between a joystick and a cursor is that the cursor moves at constant, or increasing, velocity when the

joystick is moved from its null position. If the cursor accelerates, then the acceleration is proportional to the magnitude of the joystick movement. The cursor's movement ceases once the joystick is returned to its null position.

Touchscreen
A touchscreen has an interface on the screen rendering it sensitive to touch. It returns the location of the touch. The mouse position may be controlled by tracking the position of the touch. Onscreen virtual buttons can also be realised.

Other Input Devices

Graphics Tablets
A graphics tablet may be thought of as a touchscreen without the screen. A stylus is used over a pressure sensitive surface, the co-ordinates of the pen on the surface can be determined and used in an application. The graphics tablet is never used in delivering multimedia, but it is frequently used in creating and editing multimedia objects.

Many artists find a graphics tablet preferable to a mouse for drawing objects. The tablet's stylus is held like a pen, which is a more natural action than holding a mouse. In addition, there are drawing programmes that make use of the movements that are possible with the stylus to generate different drawing effects.

Flatbed Scanners
A flatbed scanner, or more simply a scanner, is a device that captures images by scanning a linear array of light sensitive cells across a document. The scanning resolution is adjustable, so that a maximum resolution of 600 dots per inch can be achieved. Colour, monochrome or black and white data may be captured. The scanned data may be treated as an image or can be passed through optical character recognition software that will convert an image of text into the equivalent document. A scanner is seldom used in delivery systems, but rather as a means of inputting data when creating presentations.

Voice and Sound

Using a microphone and analogue to digital converter (as described in Chapter 2), sound may be input to a multimedia system. Using speech understanding software (to be described in chapter seven) the digitised speech may be "understood", rudimentary commands may be readily recognised. This topic is discussed in more detail in later chapters.

A multimedia system should also have the capability of generating or replaying captured sound. Early personal computers had a rudimentary speaker and the ability to play a small range of bleeps and buzzes. By adding a sound card, the range of sounds that could be played was increased enormously. Precaptured sound could be played: this could be music, sound effects or speech. The sound card also provided the capability of capturing sound. These days, all personal computers come equipped with a sound card.

Camera

Cameras may be either still or video, both have analogue and digital versions. Analogue cameras generate image data that must be subsequently digitised, for example the print from a still camera may be scanned using a flatbed scanner. Digital still cameras contain a certain amount of memory for limited image storage, typically 30 or so high resolution images or more lower resolution images which may be transferred directly to the computer. As we have seen, digital video requires large amounts of storage space, digital video cameras are currently limited to a few tens of minutes of recording time.

Whilst these devices are mostly used for capturing data for subsequent presentation, we shall see in later chapters how digital video is becoming more used as an input channel to systems.

Output Devices

Screen

The screen is the most common device used for presenting output from a multimedia system. It is a communication channel that is familiar to most users. The screen provides a pictorial representation of the programme's activities. The screen is driven by a video card that is responsible for converting the data it is supplied with into the correct video signals, whose characteristics were discussed in chapter two. The video card itself is driven by software modules that translate the programme's output into commands in the format understood by the video card. Fortunately, the mechanisms by which these processes occur need not be understood by multimedia systems developers.

Technologically, most screens are realised using a cathode ray tube, exactly the same as the one to be found in any domestic television receiver. However, liquid crystal displays or gas plasma displays such as those used in laptop computers are beginning to be used by desktop systems. Systems whose output is to be viewed by a large number of people simultaneously, might also utilise a video projector system. At the other extreme, systems designed for use by one person at a time have used small video screen fitted to the user's head (compare this with the virtual reality helmets that first appeared in the early 1990s). Ultimately, screen devices have been produced that project the screen image directly onto the user's retina and thereby avoid having the bulky electronics hardware necessary for driving a cathode ray tube.

Sound

The generation of sound by the computer follows the same processing stages as the display of images, but with different hardware. A loudspeaker, or pair of speakers, generates the sound. It is driven by a sound card that translates data into sounds. The data itself is translated by a sound module from the instructions it receives from the executing programme. Most sound cards in use today are capable of recording and broadcasting sound.

Kiosk Systems

Kiosk systems are a particular type of multimedia delivery system, they require minimal input from the user, but provide valuable output. They are characteristically different to the multimedia delivery systems that have been described so far because they are intended for use in public spaces. Their capabilities are therefore restricted to probably a single application.

The hardware required by a kiosk system is not necessarily different to that required by a normal multimedia system, in that they will require an output channel or channels and input channel or channels. The data channels will be specified according to the requirements of the system. This is best explained by considering two examples: a bus station enquiry kiosk and a supermarket voucher kiosk. Another kiosk system will be considered in chapter ten, that system actively surveys the scene, seeking clients it will interact with. The kiosks discussed here are essentially passive devices that respond to requests from a user.

Since kiosk systems are intended to be used by the general public, who are not necessarily computer literate, they will have additional input and output requirements. In particular, the descriptions of the required inputs must be very clear and unambiguous. The system must also be robust against erroneous or malicious input. In practice, this will mean that the input must be carefully validated.

Bus Station Enquiry Kiosk

The bus station enquiry kiosk is intended to enable bus passengers to query a timetable and route database. It is to be situated in a bus station, it is to be accessible at all times of the day, even when the manned ticket office is closed.

The system will require a keyboard for input and a screen for output, it is no different from any other multimedia system, except for the requirements that the system is accessible from outside the ticket office. The screen could be mounted inside the office, visible through a window. The keyboard must be weather and vandal proof, a membrane covered keyboard will provide weather proofing, a non-contact keyboard, again mounted inside the office would provide both weather and vandal proofing.

Supermarket Voucher Kiosk

The supermarket voucher terminal is to provide loyalty card users with recipe information and discount vouchers. The customers are to be identified from their loyalty cards; a cardreader will be used to capture this information.

Having captured the customer's identity, the kiosk takes the customer through a sequence of screens that will present current offers, and finally one screen that will offer a selection of recipes. On each screen the customer is presented with the option of printing a voucher or moving on to the next screen. Figure 4.1 illustrates the components of the system.

The physical layout of the system is important. The screen and card reader must be comfortable to use by an adult standing in front of them. As with other kiosk systems, the visible components must be robust to cope with adults and especially children.

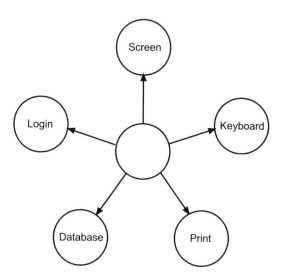

Figure 4.1 The outline architecture of the supermarket voucher kiosk

Other Systems

Kiosk systems are widely used as a means of automatically providing information. The information must be carefully selected and prepared to generate an eye catching display. The hardware used to mount the presentation must also be robust to survive intense and heavy use. The software must also be robust against misuse, inadvertent and deliberate.

Conclusions

This chapter has been concerned with the hardware requirements of a multimedia computer system. It would be very unusual for any computer that is bought today to be incapable of playing multimedia objects. So the requirements of a multimedia computer are satisfied by most off-the-shelf computers. Some additional peripheral devices may be necessary for specific tasks, for example a graphic tablet will ease the creation of original artwork.

The chapter also examined the multimedia kiosk. This is a restricted type of multimedia system suitable for deployment in public spaces. Some examples were examined.

The kiosk system provides an interesting step in the development of multimedia systems, in that they illustrate the system moving out of the laboratory or home and into an unconstrained environment. Computer systems in general are becoming ubiquitous, that is they are being installed in many more places that ever before, and used in many more applications than ever before. Apart from the need for ruggedised hardware, this requires the human-computer interface to be made simpler and easier to use. As a consequence, this necessitates a fundamental change in the nature of the interface, a screen and keyboard may no longer be appropriate, instead we might use speech input to control the system, or gestural input. The output of the system ought not to be restricted to data that can appear on a screen, the system could have speech generating capabilities, or the monitor might be replaced by an alternative type of screen.

Bibliography

Printed Material

Tannenbaum RS, (1998) *Theoretical Foundations of Multimedia*, Computer Science Press.
Vaughan T (1998) *Multimedia: Making It Work*, Osborne, Berkeley.

Internet Resources

Adobe, for Acrobat: www.adobe.com
Apple, creators of HyperCard www.apple.com
DVD: www.philips.com/pkm/laseroptics/dvd.htm and www.toshiba.com
Macromedia, creators of many drawing packages and authoring systems: www.macro-media.com
Ulead, image and video editing software: www.ulead.com

Part II

5 Multimedia Interactivity

Introduction

Multimedia systems have so far been presented as information presenting programmes. The designer of a system has some message or information to convey to his potential clients. He therefore organises this information to its best advantage, that is the way in which it is most persuasively and clearly presented. The organisational tasks will include deciding how to present each piece of information as a multimedia object and how to allow the client to navigate between the objects. The designer will use the design tools discussed in earlier chapters to integrate his objects into a coherent presentation. The tool he uses will create the presentation according to the designer's intentions. A limited amount of client interaction with the presentation is possible, just sufficient to enable the client to navigate his way through it. Whilst the format of this interactivity can appear to be sophisticated, in reality there is no more to it than selecting options by pressing a button. In essence, all currently available multimedia systems are concerned with presenting information.

Communication with most other computer systems is equally limited. The computer may convey information to the user via text, sound, or images, but the user is restricted to communicating with the computer using a keyboard and a pointing device (although some limited speech input devices are available). The situation is depicted graphically in Figure 5.1.

The limitations imposed by restricting communication to just these channels may be experienced by removing one channel from a multi-channel communication process. For example, when watching the television, one could turn off the sound or image and attempt to comprehend the programme using just the image or sound data; or during a conversation one could not watch the speaker, you would then lose all of the non-verbal cues that enhance the speaker's words.

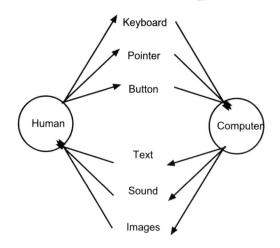

Figure 5.1 Human to computer communication channels

We must therefore ask the question, why should human to computer communication be restricted to the simple electronic channels of Figure 5.1, when human to human communications use a much larger range of channels? As suggested in Figure 5.2, when we communicate with each other, the most obvious channel we use is speech, and within this much information is contained in the way we speak, the tone of voice we use and the phrasing of sentences, changing any of these may completely change the meaning of a sentence. We also communicate using gestures: simple gestures may be used to accentuate the spoken word, or systems of gestures may become a language in their own right. Disadvantageously, being able to use many channels can also create confusion when the information conveyed by different channels is contradictory, as for example when speech and gesture contradict each other.

Multimedia systems, in addition to being able to passively capture, manipulate and deliver multimedia objects, should also be able to actively interact with their users using multiple media channels. In this chapter an overview of this topic will be presented, the following five chapters will examine different communication channels.

The Future of Multimedia Communication Systems

Currently we communicate with our computers by typing text or moving a pointing device or by clicking buttons. Voice controlled systems exist in which applications are controlled by voice command, or documents are actually dictated. At present, these systems are limited by microphone technology: the microphone must be placed close to the speaker's mouth to exclude unwanted, and probably confusing, sounds. In the future, we

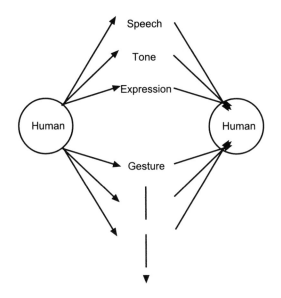

Figure 5.2 Human to human communication channels

should be able to communicate with our computers in much the same way as we communicate with each other, using speech and gestures, as well as using the "traditional" mouse and keyboard.

Applications of multimedia communication systems in the home, in the workplace (office or factory), or in public spaces may be proposed.

Homes have already been equipped with computers to provide assistance in running them. This computer can be used to control the lighting and heating, the home's security and household appliances, and entertainment systems. In fact, all of the tasks that we presently perform by controlling individual items can be controlled via one household computer. The computer can be programmed to turn the heating on and off at the correct times of the day, or turn on any cooking appliances so that food will be prepared at the required times, or to deliver entertainment to particular rooms, Figure 5.3. Such a system is programmed using a graphical interface, which can be a daunting task for some people. Figure 5.4 presents a mock-up of the interface. The interface is hosted by a single, centrally located computer.

Programming the computer, or over-riding its settings would be easier if the householder was not required to use the keyboard. Instead, the computer might be controlled by word and/or gesture from any location in the house. The computer system would have to track the householders as they moved around within the home: each person's specific requirements or computer settings would follow him or her about the house, almost as if that person's terminal were following them from room to room. For example we would not want any children in the house to be

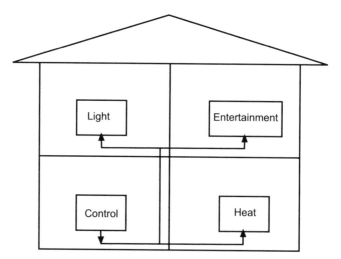

Figure 5.3 A schematic diagram of the computer controlled house. In current systems, control resides in a single computer located at a fixed point. In future systems, the interface to this computer will be accessible from any location in the house, and will follow the user as s/he moves around the house

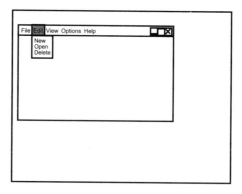

Figure 5.4 A mock-up of a graphical user interface for programming the home computer

able to control the heating system, the children would therefore be barred from accessing the heating controls.

When a person is first located within the house, the household computer must identify them. This process is analogous to logging in to a computer system. The computer will then know what tasks the person is allowed to perform and any other personal characteristics. The computer will then begin to monitor their actions. It will be seeking any recognisable gestures. For example, we may have programmed the system to turn a light on or off whenever it recognises the gesture of someone pointing at the light (provided that the gesture can be discerned when the light is off!). A working example of gesture based control was provided by Freeman at the Mitsubishi laboratories, who replaced a television remote control unit by a video based system. The system monitored the viewer for a specific gesture. When this gesture was found, the remote control interface was initialised. Further gestures then controlled the television.

The computer will also be waiting for any known words of command, again, some task will be performed once the words are recognised. In designing such a system, care must be taken that the deliberate speaking of the command is not confused with conversational use.

The system must also monitor and follow the user as he or she moves around the house, the computer will thus be aware of the locations and environments of each of its users. Therefore, if someone is listening to a radio station, the household computer will automatically reroute the signal as the listener moves between rooms. The computer will not be able to resolve any conflicts if the listener enters a room where the television is being watched.

Examples of home based multimedia systems have begun to be developed at Massachusetts Institute of Technology (MIT) and at Microsoft Research. The research programme at MIT aims to develop a computer system that is able to monitor a person's location within the room, capture and process their speech and also capture and process any gestures they might make. The system is intended to allow "computers to function as attentive human-like assistants", and has been demonstrated as an interface to a virtual pet and as a means of decoding sign language (Pentland, 1998). Microsoft's research was focussed on creating a mobile computer interface, the home was furnished with a terminal in each room, the active interface migrated from one room to another as the user moved between rooms.

Office based interfaces have been much simpler than those intended for home use. This is because the environment in which they will be used is more restricted and the tasks are less varied. Office based systems concentrated initially on multimedia communications and on replacing the mouse with simple gesture based devices.

Communication between office workers used to be face to face if this was possible, or by telephone otherwise. Given the cost of transporting personnel to meetings, the videotelephone was warmly welcomed once it became possible to base this in the working environment. This device enabled video images and sound to be exchanged between widely separated participants. It was believed that the videotelephone would revolutionise long distance communication. That this has not happened is due to the fundamental limitations of the system. In essence, the videophone consists of a monitor and a camera plus microphone and speakers. In normal, face to face conversation the participants would look at each other as they speak. Using a videophone, the participants view the monitor whilst being watched by the camera, since the monitor and camera are not coincident, neither participant looks at the other as they converse – they view the monitor rather than the camera.

Videoconferencing has been more successful than the videotelephone. The videoconference uses the same equipment as the videotelephone, the difference between the two is the number of participants. The video-conference will generally include more than one participant at each site. The distraction of the speaker not viewing his audience is therefore reduced as everyone may assume that the speaker is looking at one of the other audience members. However, videoconferencing systems suffer due to the limited amount of information that can be transmitted between sites: whilst some visual information and most sound information is adequately transmitted, the systems do lose information from the non-verbal communication channels.

Research into improving multimedia communication has been and continues to be directed towards making the equipment as unobtrusive as possible. For the videophone this might include improving the quality of the transmitted imagery, and doctoring the data to artificially increase the amount of eye contact. For the videoconference, the aim might be the create the impression that all participants are in the same location, possibly by using large video screens, certainly by carefully selecting and coding the data to be transmitted.

We might also imagine the office of the future in which the keyboard, mouse and maybe the monitor too have been replaced by alternative chan-nels. Currently researchers are investigating methods of replacing the mouse with video systems which would monitor the user's hands – hand and finger gestures would replace the mouse movements associated with pointing, clicking, click and drag etc. The workstation could be arranged as in Figure 5.5 with the video camera fixed in a position to look past the user towards the workspace. Two alternatives have been suggested. The camera could be situated behind the user and would view the monitor screen, the image would include the user's gestures and the working document which would be on-screen. Alternatively, the camera could be situated vertically above the user, the image would include the working document and any gestures made by the user over the document. The system would follow the user's hand movements and interpret them as if they were mouse movements. The key-board or a dictation system would be used to make textural changes.

Within industry, multimedia interfaces could be used to replace any interface between a worker and the equipment he is controlling.

Some interesting examples arise in the automotive industry: some car manufacturers are brave enough to suggest that gesture interfaces could be used to control some of the car's functions, but not anything critical! Instead they have been proposed as a means of opening the windows. Much effort has also been expended in developing completely autono-mous cars that are able to navigate themselves through traffic or along fixed routes. However, these are not strictly multimedia systems.

Multimedia systems deployed in public spaces were discussed in the preceding chapter, although those systems retained the "traditional"

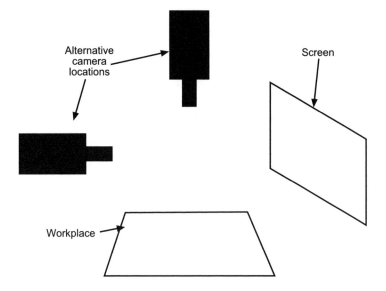

Figure 5.5 The video mouse workstation. The video camera may be situated above the user viewing a workspace on the table, or behind the user viewing the screen

keyboard and button interfaces. Kiosk systems are ideal candidates for the use of non-contact interfaces. Video input could be used to monitor the active area in front of the kiosk, this would be the area in which a client would stand to interact with the kiosk. It is assumed that a passer-by will stop in this area if they require information from the kiosk. Once a client is detected in this way, the kiosk will commence providing the information required of it.

Feedback of some form must be provided by all of these multimedia interfaces, the minimum might be some form of audible signal, a click or beep to indicate that a command had been recognised. Some systems would require more extensive feedback, such as a spoken message. This could either be delivered as a disembodied voice, or possibly from an animated character. Speech generation will be discussed in the following chapter.

Theoretical Foundations

Perceptual interfaces to computer systems are being developed. These require that multimedia information is captured by the system, processed and "understood". For a gesture based interface this will mean that gestures are identified in a stream of input data and compared with known gestures. If a match is found, then the corresponding action may be performed. For voice input, the same actions would be performed, with words replacing gestures. If this is to be achieved, what are the requirements of the systems?

A speech based multimedia system must first capture the sound data it is to process, and, equally important, it must not capture any sound that is not to be processed. This is a simple task for humans who are able to differentiate speech from ambient noise. But it is something beyond even the most sophisticated programmes. Instead, ambient noise is not captured by the system, only the required voice data is captured by placing a microphone in close proximity to the speaker's mouth.

The captured speech is divided into phonemes, separate articulations that are the building blocks of speech. Having identified the phonemes, it is generally possible to combine the sequence into meaningful data. The processes followed in doing this will be described in a following chapter.

Similarly, if text is to be converted to speech, the text is initially translated into phonemes that may be articulated. However, human speech is influenced by the emotional state of the speaker and the content of the text (expression), and each phoneme influences the pronunciation of the following one. If these factors are ignored, then the speech will sound flat, monotonous and emotionless. Again, the processes by which these factors are incorporated will be described in the following chapter.

A vision based interface must first capture the data contained in the video signal, a process that was described in an earlier chapter. It must then recognise the basic structures making up the items it is to work with. For a gesture based interface this means that the arms, hand and maybe the fingers must be isolated. For a freer interface using movement of the complete human, movement of humans must be followed.

Some systems will have input from multiple data sources, the proposed Easy Living system, and a surveillance system implemented at MIT are examples. In these interfaces, the system must be aware of the interrelationships between the data sources, such that if a "target" leaves the field of view of one data source, it must be programmed to expect the target on the field of view of one of the other data sources. The human equivalent would be expecting a person to enter one room knowing that they had just vacated an adjoining one. This problem will be revisited in chapter ten.

Some interfaces must be able to recognise a restricted number of users. Note that recognising a person is a higher level process than merely recognising that a possible target is a person. These systems will allow the recognised person to perform a defined range of tasks, for example, a home automation system should not allow all members of the household to adjust the heating system.

Having identified the target in the image, be it the user's hand or the complete user, the gestures being made must be recognised. There is a parallel with recognising speech by combining the isolated phonemes into recognisable words. Primitive gestures must also be combined into more complex gestures, compared with those gestures in a stored repository. If a match is found, then an associated action may be performed. One of the difficulties in this process is that a compound gesture may have a different interpretation to its constituents. For example, if we are creating a gesture based mouse, we would have one gesture to move the mouse and another to indicate a button click. Separately, these gestures have their own interpretations. When combined, they have a third meaning which must be reliably discriminated.

All perceptual interfaces must capture data, they must isolate primitive elements of the structure being extracted and then build a symbolic representation of the captured data. This representation will be compared against previously labelled representations that have associated meanings. The user's intention may thus be determined. All perceptual interfaces will share five fundamental requirements.

The systems must be non-contact, that is they must not require the human user to control them by direct touch, nor must they require any special apparatus to be fixed to the user. Several systems have been marketed as non-contact computer interfaces that require the operator to wear a reflective target. Such systems, whilst being effective, violate this requirement and cannot therefore be described as truly perceptual interfaces. The actual systems will be described in Chapter 7 when we consider head-pointing devices.

Second, the systems must be unobtrusive. This is a related requirement to the non-contact requirement, but deserves separate mention. Some perceptual computer interfaces require the users to wear reflective targets or other apparatus. This is not acceptable if the user is to be allowed to move about freely. Other systems will be based in the home where large or otherwise obtrusive computer equipment would not be tolerated.

Third, the systems must function in "real-time". Real-time must be interpreted according to the task being performed and the response time of the user. For most humans, any results that are presented at intervals of less than one-tenth of a second are effectively perceived as real-time, that is there is no observable delay between a user giving some input to the system and the system responding to it.

The systems being developed must be accurate. That is they must give results that are correct to some level of tolerance. The tolerance is system dependent in that some systems allow the users to automatically compensate for larger system errors than others. However, all systems must provide results that are measurably accurate.

Finally, the systems must be robust against low quality or even missing data. The system must respond predictably in these situations, compensating for erroneous data or interpolating for missing data. The system must not fail catastrophically.

Control Cycle

As with all real-time systems, these systems generally operate in two phases: an initial phase initialises the system and passes it into a second phase that performs the real-time processing. Figure 5.6 presents the high level flow of control in this system. It is initialised when the system is started, and control passes immediately to the execution module. This module performs the real-time processing of the data. In a person tracking system, the initialisation module would locate the person and assign initial values to the tracking parameters. The real-time module would perform the actual tracking. Control will pass from the real-time module when the programme is terminated, or when it loses track of its task, e.g. the person tracker loses its target. In the latter case, control will return to the initialisation module.

All multimedia interfaces are required to process significant amounts of data, more than could be exhaustively processed in the available time. We have examined the rate at which video data is generated, it is so high that no readily available processor may deliver meaningful results by processing all of the data. Instead several techniques are used to reduce the amount of data that must be processed.

The most effective approach to efficiently processing data utilises the cycle of perception, Figure 5.7. In this cycle, data is captured, it is processed and a model of the world updated. The world model is then used to direct the data capture and processing. This ensures that only relevant data is processed. For example, if a human action is being tracked, the world model might simply be a model of how the human is currently moving. This can be used to predict the human's location at any future time, with increasing uncertainty. We may therefore direct our search for the human in any image captured at a future time. Directing the search in this way effectively reduces the amount of data to be inspected and has a consequent increase in the data throughput.

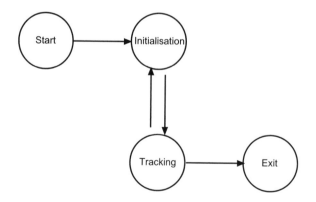

Figure 5.6 The level 0 diagram of a typical real-time interactive system

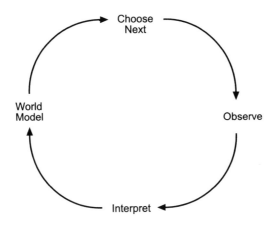

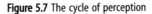

Figure 5.7 The cycle of perception

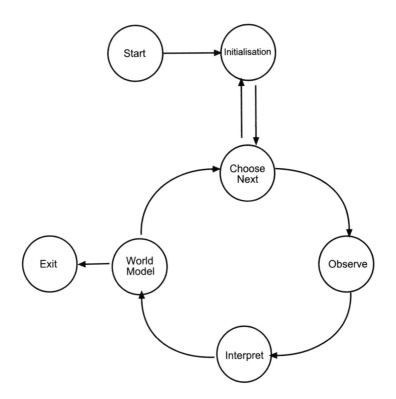

Figure 5.8 The level 0 diagram for real time control systems

Any system that operates under this model must be appropriately initialised. This process is summarised in Figure 5.8 which shows the relationship between the system running under the cycle of perception and its initialisation. Naturally the system is initialised when it is first started. But, most importantly the system must be capable of repeated initialisation as it executes, thus making it tolerant to losing data.

The software that realises such a system will be layered (Marr, 1982), as illustrated in Figure 5.9. Raw data is processed at the bottom layer and the primitive elements required for understanding are extracted. In the next layers, the primitives are combined into progressively more complex structures. The topmost layers are responsible for organising the structures into objects and recognising the objects, and also for the overall control of the system. Marr suggested that visual processes were organised in this fashion, the simplest layer of processing identified blob- or line-like elements in an image. The following layers combined the line elements into complete lines, the lines into surfaces and the surfaces into incomplete views of objects (incomplete because the furthest surfaces were obscured by the object itself). Marr proposed the scheme for visual data, but it is equally applicable to sound data. In the scheme, the flow of information is in the upward direction, there is also a downwards flow of information concerning how the data should be processed.

The following chapters are concerned with the processing of sound and visual data. The complete processing hierarchy could be presented. However, we are more concerned with discussing what tasks should be performed and outlining how they should be performed. The details of how specific image or speech processing goals are achieved are better explained in image or speech processing texts. We shall be concerned only with the topmost layers of the hierarchy.

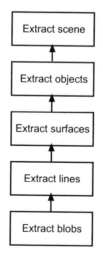

Figure 5.9 The layered architecture of a multimedia data processing module

Conclusions

The preceding chapters have described multimedia delivery systems. These are systems that have their multimedia content preprepared and organised by the designer. The user is free to peruse this data to a greater or lesser degree, depending on how it is organised. These systems are characterised by an essentially one-way flow of information, the bulk of the data flows from the computer to the users, the information flow from user to computer is minimal.

Multimedia systems are being developed in which the data flows are more equal. These systems characteristically form the interface between a user and some other computer system. In this chapter we have outlined what forms the interface might take and have looked briefly at its requirements. The following four chapters examine different types of interface in more detail, looking at voice based interfaces, alternative pointing devices, gesture interfaces and motion based interfaces.

Bibliography

Printed Material

Freeman WT, Weissman CD (1995), "Television control by hand gestures", IEEE International Workshop on Automatic Face and Gesture Recognition, Zurich, June 1995.

Holmes JN (1998) *Speech Synthesis and Recognition*, Van Nostrand and Rheinhold.

Marr D, (1982) *Vision*, Academic Press.

Jain R, Kasturi R, Schunk BG (1995) *Machine Vision*, McGraw Hill.

Pentland AP (1998) "Smart Rooms: Machine Understanding of Human Behaviour" in *Computer Vision for Human–Machine Interaction*, Cipolla R, Pentland A (eds), CUP, Cambridge.

Stroud JM (1956), "The fine structure of psychological time". In Quastler H (ed.) *Information Theory in Psychology*, Freepress, Glencoe Ill.

Wren C, Azarbayejani A, Darrell T, Pentland A, "pFinder: Real-Time Tracking of the Human Body", *IEEE Trans Pattern Analysis and Machine Intelligence*, 19:780–785.

Internet Resources

Microsoft EasyLiving: http://www.research.microsoft.com/easyliving/

MIT AI Lab's Forest of Sensors http://www.ai.mit.edu/projects/darpa/vsam/

MIT Media Laboratory: www.media.mit.edu

Mitsubishi lab's television remote control: http://www.merl.com/people/freeman/tv.html

6 Speech Generation

Introduction

Speaking computers have been present in fiction for at least 40 years, e.g. HAL in *2001*, Robbie in *Forbidden Planet*. Some had obvious computer voices, characteristically metallic and artificial, a device used to indicate that it was the computer that was speaking; others had more natural voices, HAL was one of the first of these, the voice was recognisably "human" having a natural intonation and the ability to speak with expression.

Speaking machines have actually been in existence for much longer. Early machines were mechanical devices that were designed to mimic the human vocal tract. They were curiosities and had no practical use other than to demonstrate how we produced sounds. Speech synthesis machines only became practical after the development of electrical sound recording and analysis techniques. Analysis of the frequency structure of spoken sounds gave an indication of how they could be generated artificially. Devices were produced that worked on these principles. The devices produced at this time were controlled by a human operator, who "played" the synthesiser. Automatic speech generating systems began to be developed once sufficient computing power became available in the 1970s.

Current speech synthesis systems use one of three approaches. The simplest is to simply record the segments of speech that are to be used. This limits the number of phrases or sentences that can be used, but their sound quality can be high (depending on how the recoding was performed). Alternatively, we may split the speech into its smallest components: the phonemes. In western European languages, there are less than 50 phonemes, if there were more than this number of phonemes, the approach might be impractical. A piece of text to be spoken would be translated into the sequence of phonemes and the corresponding recordings played. This approach provides complete flexibility in that any phrase may be spoken, but the quality is low because fluent speech requires fluent transition between phonemes which cannot be achieved by concatenating sequences of fixed phonemes. An approach that solves this problem is to record the transitions between phonemes rather than the phonemes themselves. The text to be spoken would still be translated into a sequence of phonemes, but the recordings to be played would differ. Current successful systems are often a hybrid of these two approaches. Small speech segments are recorded, the text to be spoken is converted into a sequence of phonemes, the appropriate recorded segments are selected and the resulting digital sound signal is manipulated to improve its realism.

Automatic speech recognition can be defined as the process by which the computer translates an acoustic signal into text. It should be understood as the reverse of speech synthesis. We can also define speech understanding, it is the process that infers abstract meaning from the text. Speech recognising systems differ according to their target application: is the system adapted to a single speaker or any speaker? How large a vocabulary will it recognise? Does it recognise continuous speech or isolated words? Speech recognising systems also differ according to the methods used to perform recognition, but all will attempt to isolate and recognise phonemes and hence to recognise the words being spoken. Chapters 6 and 7 discuss the two topics of speech synthesis and speech recognition.

The first two sections of Chapter 6 will examine human speech and present a historical review of speech synthesis systems, up to about 1980. The remaining two sections describe how a text segment may be converted into phonemes, and how natural sounding speech may be generated.

Physiology

Speech synthesis devices attempt to mimic the sounds generated by the human vocal tract which comprises the airways of the thorax and the vocal and nasal cavities in the head, Figure 6.1. Superficially, the vocal tract has similarities with many wind instruments: it has an air source (the lungs), it has a sound source (the vocal chords) and it has a resonating chamber (the throat, mouth and nasal cavities). However, musical instruments are rigid structures, the pitch of the note they produce is varied by changing the volume of the resonator, the quality of the sound cannot be changed. So a trumpet could never be confused with a clarinet. In the human vocal tract, the volume and the shape of the resonant cavity can be altered, giving a much greater degree of control over the sounds we can produce.

When we speak, air is forced from the lungs and passes through the vocal chords. Tightening or relaxing the chords allows them to vibrate with a higher or lower pitch, or to remain still. The majority of our control

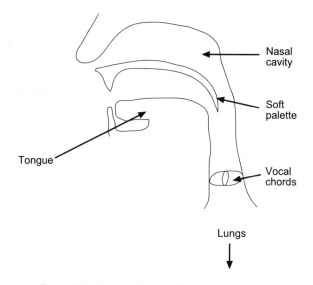

Figure 6.1 A schematic diagram of the human vocal tract

over the sounds we produce comes from our ability to change the size and shape of the vocal tract by opening the throat, moving the jaw, lips and tongue. The moveable structures are known as articulators. Whilst there is an infinite variation in the range of sounds we may produce, in all spoken languages a finite number of sounds are used as building blocks. The building blocks are known as phonemes. In western European languages, some 35 to 50 phonemes are used.

A speech signal may be transformed and viewed as a sound spectrogram. In this transform, short segments of the signal are passed through a Fourier transform which computes the frequency structure of the signal. The transformed signal is displayed as a vertical line of varying intensity. The intensity relates to the magnitude of the transform, i.e. how much energy is present in a particular frequency band. By drawing the transforms adjacent to each other we may build a representation of the changing temporal structure of the speech – the horizontal axis corresponds to time, the vertical to frequency and the intensity to the amount of sound energy in a particular frequency and time interval. Such a diagram is known as a sound spectrogram.

From the example spectrogram of Figure 6.2 we can identify several properties of phonemes. The speech giving rise to the spectrogram is displayed beneath it. Three classes of phonemes may be identified. All phonemes belong to one or a mixture of these classes.

Voiced phonemes are produced when the air expelled from the lungs causes the vocal chords to vibrate. The vibration is controlled by the tension in the vocal chords, their shape and the rate of airflow. The rate of vibration gives the pitch of the sound. Vowel like sounds are generated

Figure 6.2 A typical sound spectrogram. The vertical axis measures frequency, the horizontal axis measures time. The intensity of the graph indicates the sound energy present in that time/frequency band

in this manner. The spectrogram of the voiced phonemes contains horizontal lines, indicating significant energy content at particular frequencies. These resonant frequencies are known as formants. Although all vocal tracts are different, the formant frequencies are sufficiently constant for us to consistently recognise the voiced phonemes.

Unvoiced sounds are generated by forcing air through a constriction in the vocal tract. The vocal chords are slack and therefore do not vibrate. Sounds such as "s" and "sh" are generated. Broad band, noise like sounds result which are indicated on the spectrogram by the frequency content of the signal being uniformly and widely spread.

Third, phonemes known as plosives are generated by releasing the air blocked behind a temporary blockage of the vocal tract. "t", "b", etc. are generated by altering the position of the blockage and the shape of the articulators. The spectrogram will contain a vertical band showing no content followed by a signal that is characteristic of the plosive. Other phonemes are generated by mixtures of these processes. For example, voiced fricatives result when the vocal chords vibrate (a voiced phoneme) and the vocal tract is constricted (unvoiced phoneme).

Analysis of the spectrogram presented in this way suggests that individual phonemes exist in isolation and are constant, irrespective of their context. This is not the case, close examination of the spectrogram reveals how one phoneme merges with its preceding and succeeding neighbours. The boundaries of a phoneme are fuzzy. The reason for this is entirely physiological.

When a phoneme is spoken, the speaker changes the shape of his or her vocal tract by moving the articulators to produce the required sound.

For example, to enunciate the "ee" sound in "beet" the tongue is moved forwards and upwards. To enunciate the "a" in "father" the tongue is moved backwards and downwards and the jaw is lowered. If the "ee" and "a" are enunciated in rapid succession a smooth transition between tongue and jaw positions is made. At either end of the transition the vocal tract is in the correct position for the "ee" or "a" vowel sounds, during the transition a sound is made that does not correspond clearly to either vowel, hence the fuzzy boundaries between phonemes in the spectrogram.

A second, related difficulty arises when short vowels are uttered. In this case, the speaker has insufficient time to move the articulators into the correct configuration for the vowel before they must be moved for the following phoneme. For example, consider the "i" sounds in bill and tick, although they should sound the same, they are differently influenced by the following phonemes and therefore sound quite different. The listener is able to infer the correct phoneme from the context.

The motion of articulators between phonemes and their failure to attain the correct configuration for certain sounds is called coarticulation. The effects of coarticulation must be included in the speech model if the synthesised speech is to sound at all natural.

Historical Speech Generating Machines

The first talking machine was demonstrated in 1779 by CG Kratzenstein in Moscow. This device could make the vowel sounds by blowing air through a reed and variable resonance chamber. The different vowel sounds were made by changing the size and shape of the chamber. Twelve years later, W von Kempelen extended this device by adding further chambers to generate the consonant sounds. Careful manipulation allowed a skilled operator to produce complete utterances. Wheatstone produced an improved version in Victorian times and the last variation on this theme was in 1937 when R Riesz produced a more sophisticated version that controlled the shapes of the resonators by mechanical sliders and varied the length of the reeds to create intonation. Figure 6.3 illustrated the technique employed in these devices.

Also in the late Victorian age, Helmholtz and others, studied the relationship between a spectrum and the sound that produced it. They suggested that speechlike sounds could be produced by carefully controlling the loudness of, or amount of energy contained in, different regions of the spectrum. If this was true, then speech could be reproduced electrically instead of by mechanical reproduction of the vocal tract. Helmholtz also studied the effect of the shape of a resonant cavity on its resonant frequency. Shortly afterwards, JQ Stewart built an electrical device consisting of two coupled resonators that were periodically

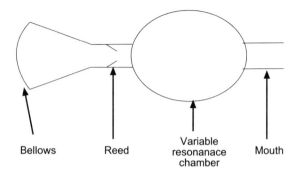

Bellows   Reed   Variable   Mouth
                               resonanace
                               chamber

Figure 6.3 An outline diagram illustrating the principle of sound generation and manipulation in the first speaking machine

excited. By tuning the resonators to different frequencies, vowel-like sounds were produced.

The electrical equivalent to von Kempelen's machine was developed in the 1930s by H Dudley, R Reiz, and S Watkins. The "Voder" was demonstrated at the World's Fair in 1939. Like von Kempelen's machine, an operator controlled the machine to produce the required sounds but the Voder used a keyboard rather than have the operator cover holes.

The Voder was not a true speaking machine, it was more like a musical instrument that could produce speechlike sounds. A true speaking machine would be presented with text and would convert it to speech. However, the Voder did demonstrate how speechlike sound could be generated electronically. The second part of the problem was how to derive the time dependent machine settings from a text.

FS Cooper, AM Liberman, and JM Borst used light to generate speech in 1951, Figure 6.4. Their device consisted of a rotating wheel of fifty concentric circles of varying opacities. (The circles were of varying opacities to accommodate the varying weights to be given to the sub-bands of the spectrum.) Light from a source was split into fifty beams that passed through the circles and on to a transparency of the spectrogram. The density of the spectrogram blocked more or less of each beam. Beyond the spectrogram the beams were recombined and directed to a photoelectric cell whose output was amplified and fed into a loudspeaker. The sound so generated was an accurate representation of the pictorial representation of the speech. The machine was ultimately a failure as a speech generator, as it took a previously analysed speech segment as its input – it recorded and played back the speech. It did however demonstrate that speech could be generated from time varying parameters, even if the fifty parameters they used were too complex to be of practical use.

Returning to Helmholtz's resonator experiments, recall that it was possible to produce speechlike sounds with a pair of coupled resonators. By changing the resonant frequencies, different speech sounds could be

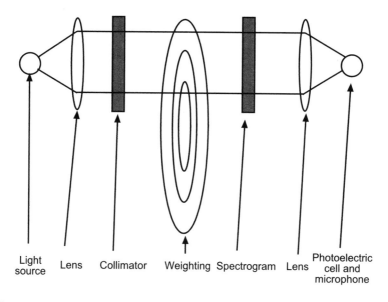

| Light source | Lens | Collimator | Weighting | Spectrogram | Lens | Photoelectric cell and microphone |

Figure 6.4 A diagram illustrating the principle of Cooper, Liberman and Borst's voice synthesiser

produced, as the resonances corresponded to the formant frequencies of different phonemes. Many researches have worked on the problems of determining the formant frequencies of phonemes, and of predicting how the formant frequencies will change over time in a given phoneme sequence. If those problems were solved, a speaking machine could be developed. Two methods of deriving a solution have been defined: synthesis from stored samples and synthesis by rule.

Synthesis from Stored Segments

The easiest method of producing computer speech is to store small segments of human speech and replay them as required. For example, digital telephone exchanges can pass on information such as the number of your last caller: a human voice was recorded speaking each digit and any other messages that might be needed. When information is requested, the exchange will play the recordings corresponding to the appropriate message; if a telephone number is requested, the digit recordings are played in succession.

This example reveals the shortcomings of this approach. The number of recordings that can be stored is severely limited by the amount of storage available for the digitised data. Thus the number of utterances that can be made is limited to the number of single recordings and sensible combinations of multiple recordings. The quality of the reproduced speech is as good as the recording, except when recordings are combined. In this case the speech sounds stilted because our pronunciation of a word changes according to the words before and after it and this application is enunciating the words as if they were spoken in isolation.

If synthesising speech from recorded words or phrases is not viable, is it possible to synthesise it from smaller building blocks? We saw above, that speech is composed of sequences of phonemes, is it therefore possible to synthesise realistic speech by combining the required phonemes? Such an approach is very attractive as the number of phonemes is small (less than about 50), they are of short time duration, implying that the storage requirements are modest, but an entire language may be synthesised from them.

Having a small number of phonemes makes their use attractive. However, coarticulation means that they are too variable in normal speech for them to be useful, a computer speech system that used phonemes would sound extremely stilted. A viable alternative would be to use the transitions between phonemes as the building blocks for speech. These transitions would capture the coarticulations between neighbouring phonemes. The transitions are known as diphones and they are defined formally to start at the middle of a phoneme and end at the middle of the following one. A speech segment may therefore by synthesised by concatenating a sequence of diphones. Care must be taken to match the diphones across the joins, differences in loudness and spectral characteristics are obvious as clicks and other unwanted sounds in the speech segment.

Speech synthesis systems are usually assessed using two quality criteria. The first is intelligibility: can the synthesised speech be understood? The second criterion is naturalness: does the synthesised speech mimic the characteristics of a human speaker, or could the speech synthesiser be mistaken for a human? If we synthesise speech by concatenating primitive elements, then the speech will be more or less accurate, it will certainly be intelligible, but it will not sound at all natural as it will lack inflection and expression. Some applications and users will tolerate intelligible but unnatural speech, other applications or users will require intelligible and natural speech. The problem of making synthetic speech sound natural is discussed in the following section.

Synthesis from Rules

The problem of converting a piece of written text into a natural sounding spoken representation may be divided into two stages. The first is to transform the written text into a sequence of phonemes and to derive the accentual parameters. The second problem is to transform the linguistic parameters into parameters that can drive the generation of speech. Figure 6.5 illustrates the process, the text must be divided into

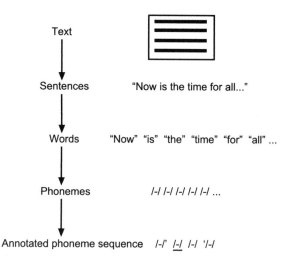

Text

Sentences   "Now is the time for all..."

Words   "Now" "is" "the" "time" "for" "all" ...

Phonemes   /-/ /-/ /-/ /-/ /-/ ...

Annotated phoneme sequence   /-/' /-/ /-/ '/-/

Figure 6.5 Steps in the process of synthesising speech from text. The input text is divided into sentences, words and phonemes before being annotated with an indication of the intonations to be used. The individual phonemes may be converted to digital sounds, and the resulting signal is manipulated to reflect coarticulation and intonation

segments corresponding to sentences, words and phonemes. Indications of the accenting, pauses and stresses are added. The resulting annotated phonemes are then converted into a digital speech signal that must be manipulated to obscure the joints and add colour and texture before playing it the a digital to analogue converter.

Transforming Text to Linguistic Parameters

The aim of this process is to take a string of text, to convert it to an annotated sequence of phonemes. The annotations will indicate which phonemes are to be stressed, how the pitch and pace of the speech is to be controlled, etc. The process is commonly divided into five stages: normalisation, tokenisation, word pronunciation, accentuation and prosodic phrasing. Each stage requires an intimate knowledge of the language being spoken.

Normalisation

Normalisation is a preprocessing step that converts the input textural data into the sequence of words that would be spoken. Several tasks will be performed: abbreviations will be expanded, acronyms and numbers will be transformed into the correct word format. Some reordering of words may be performed. Also, since most speech synthesisers process complete sentences, Normalisation will also divide the input text into discrete sentences.

Consider the sentence "Good morning, Dr. Morris". To normalise this text, the system must know that Dr. expands to doctor in this sentence because Morris is a person's name. If "Dr." followed a proper noun it would expand to "Drive": a road name. The normalised text would be "good morning doctor Morris".

Reordering is often necessary when normalising amounts of money. Thus "£5 thousand" would be normalised to "five thousand pounds", and not "pound sign five thousand". Similarly, "£5M" would be normalised to "five million pounds".

The result of Normalisation is that the input text has been divided into its constituent sentences, all of the non-word characters and abbreviations have been expanded, and the resulting text reordered as necessary. The normalised text is simply the sequence of words that would be spoken when reading the input text.

Tokenisation

Tokenisation is the process of dividing the normalised text into its constituent words. For English and many other languages, this is a straightforward task as words are separated by punctuation marks or white space.

For other languages, most notably Chinese, the task is considerably more difficult. Chinese characters correspond to monosyllables, a word may be composed of more than one character and characters in a paragraph are written with no intervening white space. Paragraphs are separated by white space. Heuristic and statistical approaches to tokenisation have been attempted. Heuristically methods have found the longest word at the head of the input string. Statistical methods have been used to find the most probable sequence of words from the input string. Whichever approach has been taken, the Tokeniser must be supplied with a dictionary since it must know when it has read a word. The Tokeniser must also be equipped with methods of recognising derived words, personal names or foreign words transliterated into Chinese.

Word Pronunciation

Having tokenised the sentence, we may make a first attempt at computing a pronunciation for the words. A simple approach is to employ a set of rules that define the sound equivalents of the letters. The rules are used to translate the sequence of letter symbols into a sequence of phonemes and possible stress information. Again, this is easier for some languages than others: Welsh and Spanish for example are written phonetically and there is a close and consistent relationship between the written symbols and the corresponding sounds. English is notoriously inconsistent in its pronunciations, having numerous homophones and word segments with the same spelling but different pronunciations. A pronunciation dictionary is necessary, at least for those words whose pronunciation cannot be predicted using the letter-to-sound rules. The problem noted above will occur when using a pronunciation dictionary: it will not include derived words nor personal names.

A pronunciation for a morphologically derived word may be computed from the pronunciation of the constituent parts. For example, the word "morphology" is derived by combining "morph" and "ology". If we know how to pronounce the constituents, we may simply combine their pronunciations. Other pronunciations may be estimated by analogy, knowing how to pronounce morphology, the may make a sensible guess at the pronunciation of geology.

The same methods may be applied to the pronunciation of proper names. In addition, a proper name may have a foreign origin, in which case it should be pronounced according to its language of origin. The original language must be guessed by inspecting the name, typically the frequency of occurrence of combinations of letters will suggest a language.

In many languages there are words with the same spelling but different pronunciations. These rules can be applied to such words and they will return a set of possible pronunciations. For example, the word "bass" could be a fish or a musical range. The correct pronunciation is determined by the word's context. If nearby words musically related, then they will decide the pronunciation. Compare how we normalised the abbreviation "Dr.", if it was before a name, it expanded to "doctor", and after a name it expanded to "drive".

Accentuation

In most languages, various words in a sentence can be accented, that is they are spoken with an upwards or downwards shift in the fundamental frequency. A statement can be changed to a question by raising the pitch of the voice towards the end of the sentence.

An initial assignment of accents may be made on the basis of lexical categories. Content words such as nouns, verbs and adjectives could be accented. Function words: auxiliary verbs and prepositions are unaccented. Obviously the input sentence must be parsed to determine the accenting.

A more complex form of accenting is associated with the pronunciation of noun phrases (a noun preceded by one or more modifiers). In most phrases then accenting is not predictable, Chorlton Street and Oxford Road place the accents differently.

Prosodic Phrasing

The methods discussed so far may be applied to short sentences with no difficulty. But speakers or writers often generate longer, more complex sentences by concatenating simpler constructs. When speaking such a sentence, the reader would naturally break it into the simpler constructs and treat each as a separate intonational unit or prosodic phrase. If there is much punctuation in the sentence, then the sentence may be divided at the commas, semicolons and full stop into its prosodic phrases. But if the sentence lacks punctuation, where should the breaks occur?

One suggestion is to have a list of words whose location signifies a breakpoint although these must be used carefully. Function words are usually a good choice, but can give particularly bad phrasing. If, for example, we used the word "and": "I went shopping and I bought a hammer and nails".

Conclusion

This section has discussed methods of transforming textural data into an annotated phoneme sequence. This contains the basic speech sounds to be made and an indication of the changing pitch, accent and intonation that will add meaning and naturalness to the utterance. This is the data that the speech generator will convert to sounds.

Generating Speech

Most languages have a well defined phoneme set, so the phonemes that are input to the speech generator are associated unambiguously with specific sounds. However, sounds that are spoken do not always correspond to the phonemes that are written: sometimes phonemes are distorted because of coarticulation, sometimes they are changed completely. To enhance the synthesised speech's naturalness, the speech generator must first identify what phonemes ought to be modified and how. This is achieved using sets of rules derived for regions and countries.

Speech is generated by transcribing the annotated phoneme sequence into the flow of parameters that control the synthesiser. These parameters will include the fundamental vocal frequency, the duration of each speech segment. The speech synthesiser will also be able to give the synthetic speech a variable intensity and timbre, these can be used to give character to the speech. Intonational and a duration models are also needed to control the synthesiser.

Common synthesisers are rule based, in that the parameters are set according to the input. Thus the fundamental frequency, the duration of a sound are given initial values according to the phoneme sequence. The values can be varied to control the accent of the synthesised voice. The values should also be modified according to their context, i.e. one phoneme ought to influence its neighbours, it should also be possible to modify the utterance of a word within a sentence, to reflect that word's significance. Therefore, multiple instances of the same word in a single sentence will be given different sounds.

At this stage of the synthesis, we have derived the time varying para-meters that will actually control the synthesiser. The final step of synthesis is to actually create the waveform. This may be achieved using one of three techniques: synthesis of formants, concatenating speech segments or synthesis by model.

Articulatory Synthesisers

This type of synthesiser uses a physiologically based model of speech production. It will include the kinematics and locations of the articulators during each phase of the production of a speech sound. The sound radi-ated from the speaker's mouth can thus be computed. Not surprisingly, such synthesisers have not found widespread acceptance due to the computational cost involved and the as yet unresolved problems of modelling the vocal tract.

Formant Synthesis

These synthesisers use a descriptive approach to synthesis. The main features of the speech signal are modelled for each sound that may be produced. So if an "aa" phoneme is to be generated, the synthesiser will generate the appropriate formant signals. Similarly for the other formants. The combination of signal segments is controlled by a rule base which may contain several hundred rules. High quality synthesised speech may be generated using this approach.

Concatenating Speech Segments

Concatenative synthesisers are probably the simplest type of speech synthesisers. They use short speech segments that are assembled into the required utterance. The segments may be diphones (phoneme to phoneme transitions), syllables or even whole words. The synthesiser translates the phoneme sequence into a sound unit sequence. The resulting waveform must be processed so as to reduce the effect of any possible discontinuities at the joints, and to make the resulting signal match any required voice more closely.

Summary

Computers can be made to speak using one of three methods. The simplest is to record the voice of a human speaking the desired words or phrases. This approach can generate high quality speech (depending on how much care was taken in recording the samples) but is limited in the amount of speech that can be generated. We have also seen how speech can be generated by concatenating sequences of phonemes, the basic speech building blocks. In European languages there is a small number of different phonemes. Speech may be generated by recording samples of phonemes and replaying these in the correct order. However, this approach runs into the problem of coarticulation – the variation in to the pronunciation of a phoneme caused by the articulators recovering from the previous one or preparing for the next.

A simple method of avoiding the coarticulation problem is to build speech from the transitions between phonemes, the diphones. In a language of fifty phonemes, there will be 2500 diphones. The same approach is taken towards translating text to speech, the phoneme boundaries are identified, and the speech building blocks recognised.

Once a piece of text has been converted to a sequence of diphones, it could be "spoken". This would result in unattractive, monotonic speech. The synthesiser must first add emphasis and inflection. To achieve this, the generator must normalise the text, it must divide it into phrase groups and it must decide where the emphasis is to be placed. These tasks imply that the synthesiser must, at least, partially understand the text.

Bibliography

Internet Resources

Comp.speech FAQ: http://svr-www.eng.cam.ac.uk/comp.speech
HAL's Legacy: http://mitpress.mit.edu/e-books/Hal/contents_java.html
Online Museum of Speech Analysis and Synthesis: http://mambo.ucsc.edu/psl/smus/smus.html

7 Speech Recognition

Introduction

Recognising spoken words is a difficult problem. A well known example illustrates this. If I said:

"Let's talk about how to wreck a nice beach."

It would be meaningful to a small group of people but most would not appreciate the sentiment. The same sentence would be more understandable if it was interpreted as:

"Let's talk about how to recognise speech."

The lesson to be learnt from this example is that speech is understood in context. Spoken language is notoriously ambiguous, it is only our understanding and knowledge of the situation, the subject matter and the person speaking that lets us understand what is being said. The process of understanding is not the passive set of actions that we often take it to be, we do not capture sound, process it and then comprehend the meaning. Instead, we build up possible meanings as we progress, and predict what words will follow. This allows us to automatically correct mistakes made by the other person, to fill in gaps that we may have misheard and to predict the ends of sentences. This type of process is called "hypothesis and test", as one processes a segment of speech, one hypothesises the most likely meaning and therefore the most likely words to follow and tests the hypothesis against the words that one hears. Sometimes the test part is omitted and misunderstandings occur.

Speech recognition systems are characterised by several parameters. First, is the system intended to recognise isolated words, or continuous speech. Recognition of isolated words is a simpler problem, and systems that do this have a limited range of applications; how often do we speak with silences between words?

Second, systems are characterised by their ability to recognise spontaneous or scripted speech. Speech read from a prepared script will be

grammatically correct, whereas spontaneous speech is notoriously inaccurate. Underlying a speech recognition system will be a model of the
language it is to recognise. Building the model is easier if the language
to be recognised is known to adhere to clearly defined grammatical rules.
One measure of the sophistication of the language model is its perplexity.
This is defined as the average number of words that may follow any single
word, values range from less than ten to above 100.

Third, systems are designed to be speaker independent or speaker
dependent. There are inter and intra speaker differences in enunciation,
arising from national are regional accents, physiological differences
between speakers and an individual's physical and emotional state.
Speaker independent systems are able to adapt to the speech patterns of
different users. Speaker dependent systems require the user to train them
by speaking predefined utterances.

This chapter will first describe two general principles underlying
speech understanding systems and will then discuss the practical
methods of implementing a system, processing the acoustic data and
recognising the phonemes, groups of phonemes and words themselves.
In many ways, speech understanding should be viewed as the reverse of
speech generation: generation transforms a written text to a sound signal,
recognition performs the reverse.

Principles Underlying Speech Recognition

Two principles define the problem of speech recognition. First, recognising
speech is a difficult problem because of the intrinsic variability of speech
waveforms and the content of the speech (there are many ways of saying
the same thing). The consequence of this variability is the amount of
domain knowledge that must be employed to solve the problem.

Speech is Unpredictable

The speech recognition system must be capable of reliable performance
despite the huge variation in normal speech patterns. Consider the differences between different people's utterances of the same word, or even
one person's utterances of the word at different times and under different
conditions. Despite this variability, human listeners recognise the same
word and we also expect computer based systems to.

If humans are able to decode this variability, there must be some
features of the audio signal that are constant. Extensive study of spec-
trograms reveals that there are invariant features associated with all
phonemes. For example, vowel sounds are made by combining one, two
or three resonant frequencies, or formants, in varying proportions. Vowel
sounds may therefore be identified by recognising the relative amounts

of each formant. Other phonemes may be identified by isolating other invariants.

The loudness of the speech may alter between and within utterances. Whilst the loudness may be indicative of the speaker's emotional state, it does not contribute anything to the meaning of the utterance. Any audio signal should therefore be normalised for loudness prior to analysis.

Not only does a speaker vary the loudness of his voice, the speed with which he speaks also changes, between utterances, within utterances, even within words. It has been observed that the duration of some phonemes is constant, i.e. the plosive consonants ("p", "b", "t"), whilst the duration of others (the vowels) changes to accommodate the change of speed. If speech recognition is being performed by comparing the sample against a template, the sample and template might never make a perfect match. The time axis of the sample must be expanded or contracted to achieve a match.

Speech Knowledge

A speech recognising system must encode many different types of knowledge (Fig. 7.1): ranging from the structure of speech sounds to the rules of grammar, plus an understanding of the dialogue that is being processed. Each level builds on the previous, less specific level. Thus, underpinning every system, and independent of what language is being processed, we must build in knowledge of how speech is produced and the types of sounds we will be processing. This will allow us to extract from the audio signal the primitive elements of the speech data – the phonemes, as discussed in Chapter 6.

The next level, the dialect/language rules define the possible orderings of the phonemes. Phonemes do not appear in any ordering, as many sequences either cannot be articulated (e.g. ptkee) or are not present in the language being processed. The set of valid phoneme sequences is further reduced as many sequences do not correspond to valid words of the language. It is interesting to note that the set of phonemes is largely language independent, i.e. a similar set of basic linguistic building blocks is used in all languages.

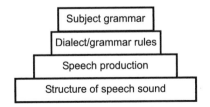

Figure 7.1 The layers of knowledge in speech recognition

The penultimate layer of knowledge involves specific grammar rules of the language being spoken. The previous layers will define the sounds that the speech processor will recognise, the possible orderings of the sounds in valid words or word segments. This layer will define the valid orderings of words in the sentences being spoken. In some instances, this knowledge may be used by parsing the input sentence, although spoken language is so ambiguous that the results of parsing may be of limited use. In fact, without even higher levels of knowledge, parsing may be impossible. Consider the sentence "Time flies like an arrow". The sentence may be parsed, but its meaning can still be unclear, possible interpretations are:

1. Time passes quickly.
2. Time the passage of the flies in the same way that an arrow times flies.
3. Time the passage of those flies that resemble arrows.
4. 'Time flies' (whatever they are) are fond of arrows.

The highest level knowledge in the speech recognising system will contain the information that is required to disambiguate the meaning of sentences such as this example. Incorporating this knowledge will begin to turn the speech recognising system into a speech understanding one. The necessity for including this layer in a speech recognition system illustrates the complexity of the process. In the case of this example, the system would have to know that there is no such object as a 'time fly', flies do not resemble arrows and an arrow cannot be a timing device; only the first interpretation is valid.

In addition to the general rules of language, this layer will also have to include knowledge about the specific topic being discussed. In fact, it is this knowledge that can make a speech recogniser successful in a specific domain, if the language used in that domain is sufficiently restricted.

Architecture of a Speech Recognition System

A typical speech recognition system will perform the operations illustrated schematically in Figure 7.2. It will take a speech signal as input and output a sequence of token that indicate the words it has recognised. The three stages of the processing are representation, classification and recognition.

Representation is simply the process that converts the analogue acoustic signal to a digital version. It is followed by classification, the process that extracts pattern information from the signal. Speech signals contain information concerning the words being spoken and the speaker. The classification process will extract the information useful for recognising words and

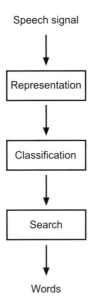

Speech signal

Representation

Classification

Search

Words

Figure 7.2 The schematic architecture of an archetype speech recognition system

suppress the speaker specific information. Finally, recognition will attempt to recognise the stream of patterns as a meaningful sequence of words.

Representation

The human auditory system is very well trained to understand speech, infants spend several years learning how to understand speech and to speak. If the captured speech is to be listened to by humans, then it can be of poor quality: data sampled to eight bit resolution at a rate of 8 kHz is sufficient, the quality of the recording will be low, but it will be understandable. Automatic speech processing requires data of a better quality.

The input to the speech recognition system is a digitised segment of speech. The acoustic waveform will have been digitised at a rate of between 6.6 kHz and 20 kHz. It is usual to sample the data to 12 bit resolution and to use a linear analogue to digital converter.

Classification

The goal of acoustic signal processing is to prepare the data for identifying the speech. This will include identifying the beginning and ending of an utterance, normalising the data for its loudness and then extracting the speaker invariant parameters that will allow phoneme identification to take place.

Having captured the data, the start and end points of the speech portions must be identified. Finding these points accurately is a non-trivial task due to the non-speech noises that will also be captured. However, reasonable results are obtained by looking at the energy content of the signal, or the rate of zero crossings. The energy content of the data is estimated by computing the average squared amplitude in a small window, if the measured amplitude exceeds a predefined threshold then speech data is present. Similarly, if the number of zero-crossings in the window exceeds a threshold, speech data is present (a zero crossing occurs when the level of the audio signal changes from positive to negative or vice versa).

In the previous chapter, the spectrogram was used to illustrate the properties of phonemes. It is not surprising therefore that the spectrogram is used to derive features that will in turn be used to identify the words in the speech segment.

The short term power spectrum (STPS) of the signal is computed from overlapping segments of the signal, each about 25 ms long. The segments are windowed (as described in Appendix 2) and passed through a Fourier transform. The resulting transform data is resampled to twenty values by comparing the data against nineteen thresholds. The thresholds are non-uniformly distributed, to reflect the frequency response of the human ear. Finally, the logarithm of the spectrum's modulus is computed. The process is summarised in Figure 7.3. This algorithm has thus reduced a short segment of the speech signal to a set of twenty parameters.

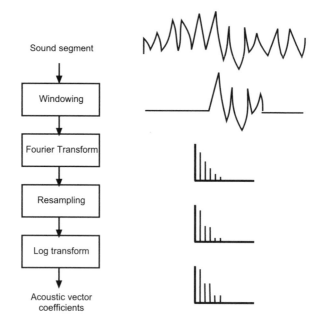

Figure 7.3 Summary of the algorithm for computing the acoustic pattern vectors

The values of the adjacent parameters are likely to be correlated. That is, one parameter is likely to have a similar value to its neighbours. The consequence of this is that although we have twenty parameters, the information could be represented with a smaller number of uncorrelated parameters. Several methods of decorrelating the data exist, one of the most widely used is to take their discrete cosine transform (DCT, defined in Appendix 2) and select the most significant coefficients. Approximately half of the coefficients will remain, but they are sufficient to represent the segment of the speech signal. These coefficients are known as cepstral coefficients.

Recognition

Cepstral filtering will have removed almost all of the speaker's characteristics from the audio signal. The remaining information will be due mostly to the speech data. The recognition process will receive a stream of pattern vectors (the cepstral coefficients) and will attempt to map them to meaningful sequences of words. Labelling of the sound data is a difficult task due to the variability of the data. Two commonly used alternatives are cochlea modelling and statistical methods using Hidden Markov Models.

Cochlea Modelling

Cochlea modelling is a simple technique that can be used to develop isolated word, single speaker speech recognition systems. Because we are interested in developing a restricted use system, the inter speaker variability will not occur. We may therefore ignore methods of reducing the variability and can process the spectrogram directly.

Cochlea modelling attempts to recognise words using a mechanism broadly similar to the cochlea's. Recall that in the ear, sound energy is converted in the cochlea into nerve signals that are frequency coded. That is, the cochlea can be viewed as a bank of band pass filters (Fig. 7.4). The same effect may be realised in the spectrogram data by dividing it into horizontal bands. The data is also divided into small time segments. The amount of energy in each time-frequency segment is summed, Figure 7.5. This sequence of measurements is characteristic of the word or phrase being spoken and can therefore be used to recognise individual words or short phrases.

The recognition process will require that samples of the words to be recognised have been previously captured. We will therefore have estimates of the words to be recognised and their variabilities. The word to be recognised may be compared to all of the estimates and classified as the most similar word. This method is really only suitable for short

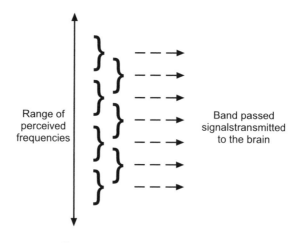

Figure 7.4 Band pass filtering in the cochlea

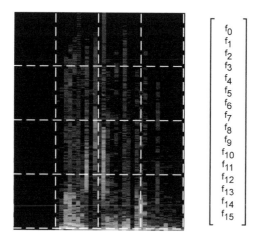

Figure 7.5 A feature vector derived from the spectrogram according to the cochlea model

samples, single, isolated words are probably best, otherwise the measurement vectors become too long and their intrinsic variation too large to make reliable recognition possible.

Hidden Markov Models

A more sophisticated approach that is suitable for recognising continuous speech is to extract the cepstral coefficients from the signal and use the sequence of coefficient vectors to build up an estimate of the words being uttered. A statistical technique known as hidden Markov modelling is the method of choice for this task.

In speech recognition, a pattern vector is generated once every 10 to 25 ms. Sequences of these vectors are to be recognised as words or word units and, eventually, as sequences of words. Recognition is a difficult process due to the inherent variability of the utterances: a word is pronounced differently by different people and by the same person at different times. The variation can include changing the pronunciation of phonemes and the pace at which a word is spoken. Hidden Markov models are powerful enough to capture these variations and represent them with sufficient flexibility to allow matching to occur using dictionaries of tens of thousands of words.

A hidden Markov model (HMM) is composed of two random processes: a hidden Markov chain and an observable process. The Markov chain, which cannot be directly observed, can be used to represent the spoken utterance. The observations are represented by the sequences of acoustic pattern vectors. The Markov chain is a linked set of states, we may move between states in this model according to the observations.

The model is represented by a number of parameters:

$A = \{a_{ij}\}$, the set of probabilities of there being transitions between states i and j;

$B = \{b_{ij}\}$, the set of output distributions, that is the probability of making a given observation given that the model was in state i and is now in state j; and

$\Pi = \{\pi_i\}$, the initial probability of the model being in the first state of this chain.

A sample of a discrete HMM is shown in Figure 7.6 The discrete model is a special case in which the elements of B are probability distributions of discrete (rather than continuous) variables. For this example, we have a matrix of transition probabilities:

$$A = \begin{bmatrix} 0.6 & 0.4 & 0.0 \\ 0.0 & 0.7 & 0.2 \\ 0.0 & 0.0 & 0.0 \end{bmatrix}$$

and for each transition, there is a distribution of the variables, as shown against the corresponding arc in the figure.

The HMM of a word or speech unit will be built by examining many samples of the pronunciation of the word or speech unit. In general, the number of states in the model will be proportional to the time duration of the utterance, since samples are generated at a fixed rate. The number of transitions between different states will be related to the number of phonemes in the word. Transitions from one state to the same one will allow the recogniser to process the same word being spoken at a different tempo, a slower tempo will result in longer sequences of the same pattern vector and hence transitions from one state back to the same one. For simplicity, most HMMs do not allow transitions between states for which

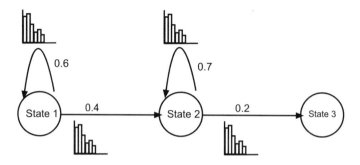

Figure 7.6 Example of a discrete hidden Markov model

$j > i$ or $j > i + 2$. That is transitions that correspond to returning to an earlier state are not allowed, neither are transitions that leapfrog intermediate states.

Having computed the HMM for a word, how is it used in recognition?

Each sequence of acoustic patterns is compared with the HMM for each word in the recogniser's dictionary. This will result in a probability that the captured sequence is compatible with a sequence that could be generated by each of the models. The computation of the probabilities of each word is computed in parallel, the initial probabilities are defined by Π, thereafter the next speech pattern vector can be used to update the probabilities according to the HMMs. Initially, there will be a large number of models to be considered, the number will equal the number of words in the recogniser's dictionary. However, many of the probabilities will rapidly fall to negligibly small values and those models need no longer be considered. At the end of the utterance, either one or a small collection of the n-best words will be generated. Linguistic models may be used to resolve any conflict.

A linguistic model attempts to set likelihood values to the probabilities of observing specific combinations of words. Since it would be impossible to generate values for the infinite number of sentences that could be spoken, most recognisers are restricted to representing the probabilities of two or three word sequences (which is still a large number of values). As shown in Figure 7.7, the language can be represented as a (very large) transition matrix between all pairs of words in the recogniser's dictionary. The nodes of the graph correspond to the words in the dictionary, the arcs are labelled with the probabilities of observing such a transition.

If we were to include the HMMs that represent the individual words into this graph, then the resulting structure would become one huge HMM which may be traversed in a search for the best interpretation of the data. Due to its size, the graph cannot be searched exhaustively, tree search methods can be adopted which will find a good solution, but not necessarily the best one.

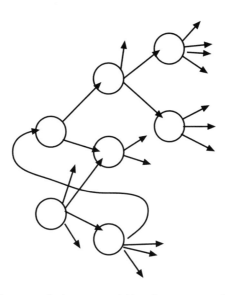

Figure 7.7 An extract of a language model based on sequences of two words

Summary

Speech recognition is a difficult task made soluble by incorporating knowledge about the methods used by humans to generate and recognise speech: how phonemes are produced and how they are grouped in to words. Any speech recogniser will first isolate the speech regions of the captured audio signal – there is little point in recognising silence! Segments of the resulting speech data are then passed through a short term Fourier transform to discover the evolution of the signal's frequency structure. Inter speaker variability may be removed, or reduced, by cepstral filtering. This transform takes the logarithm of the transformed data, quantises it into a smaller number of bins and passes the resulting values through a discrete cosine transform. A smaller number of coefficients may be used to represent the original data.

Two speech recognition methods were examined: cochlea modelling which is appropriate for recognising individual words and Hidden Markov Modelling which is suitable for continuous speech recognition. Significant problems remain to be solved before automatic speech recognition systems are able to match human performance.

Humans are able to understand speech even when the speech signal is masked by environmental noise. No techniques have yet been developed to divide the digitised acoustic signal into the required speech and the non-required noise. The performance of speech recognition systems is therefore poor when the data is adversely affected by environmental noise.

Many systems are also unable to deal with the features that characterise spontaneous speech, such as hesitations and false starts. Indeed, any feature that cannot be represented in a linguistic model will confuse the recogniser, this will also include any words that have not been included in the model.

Current systems are also poor at inter-speaker adaptation. A system that has been trained to recognise one speaker's utterances, will generally perform badly when a second speaker uses it.

Current research in this topic is addressing all of these problems. Alternative representations of acoustic features are being sought. The wavelet transform and artificial neural networks show promise, as do methods that attempt to discover articulations from the speech patterns. This last method would be useful as it would allow a robust and compact representation of the speech pattern.

Other researchers are attempting to improve language models to incorporate the features of spontaneous speech and to make systems capable of adapting between speakers.

Bibliography

Internet Resources

Comp.speech FAQ: http://svr-www.eng.cam.ac.uk/comp.speech
HAL's Legacy: http://mitpress.mit.edu/e-books/Hal/contents_java.html

8 Head Pointing Devices

What is a Head Pointing Device?

A head pointing device is a peripheral device that uses head movements to replace the mouse. It may appear in many guises, this chapter will focus on two types: the eye mouse and the head joystick.

An eye mouse is a multimedia peripheral device in which the user's direction of gaze is used to direct the on-screen cursor, instead of the more usual hand-operated mouse. The system will move the cursor to the point on the screen that the user is looking at. The system has certain restrictions, the main one being that the user must direct his gaze consistently at the screen, if he looks away for any reason the system's behaviour will become somewhat erratic.

A closely related, but conceptually different system is the head joystick, in this the attitude of the user's head is used to direct the movement of the cursor. When the user directs his head straight at the screen the cursor remains stationary, when the user inclines his head downwards, the cursor moves downwards and continues to move until the user returns his head to the straight-ahead position. This method of driving the cursor is less demanding as the user can look away from the screen without the cursor's behaviour becoming unpredictable and, more importantly, the system need not be as accurate as the eye-mouse since the user is able to continually update the direction of the cursor's movement.

The eye mouse and head joystick systems find numerous applications, ranging from a replacement of the mouse for able bodied and disabled users to interfaces to active three dimensional displays (these are often used for information delivery in public spaces). This chapter will discuss examples of these uses, it will also describe alternative methods of replacing the mouse and early attempts at decoding a user's gaze direction. The bulk of the chapter is, however, concerned with the implementation of non-contact, video based eye and head pointing devices.

Several systems have been produced that actively illuminate the user with infra red light. This is reflected from the retina and is seen as a highlight in the video image. Due to the shape of the eye's surface, the highlight is offset from the centre of the iris by an amount proportional to the angle between the direction of gaze and the illumination source. The direction of the offset is opposite to the direction of gaze. These systems will locate the bright reflections in the image – there will be one from each eye and no others, and will attempt to find the boundary between the iris and the white of the eye. The relative locations of the highlight and iris boundary determine the direction of gaze to a high degree of accuracy and therefore allow the eye-mouse to be implemented. However, this chapter is concerned with how head pointing devices would be implemented using video techniques.

Where Would Head Pointing Devices Be Used?

A head pointing device could be used to replace a mouse in any situation where hands free operation was required. The most obvious use is as a communication aid for the disabled. It could also be used as an aid for controlling other devices when the users' hands were otherwise engaged, such a device has been suggested for keyhole surgeons. A less obvious use is to control active holographic displays.

For many people with physical disabilities, computers form an essential tool for communication, environmental control and entertainment. However access to the computer may be made more difficult by a person's disability. A number of users employ head-operated devices in order to interact with a computer. The device would typically include a sensor worn on the user's head connected to the computer via a suitable interface. The sensor is intended to measure the user's head orientation and the interface is designed to convert the measurement into a cursor control command (e.g. up or down, left or right). A range of imaginative solutions to the problem of measuring the head orientation have been suggested, ranging from Hall effect switches (which measure the Earth's magnetic field) attached to eyeglasses, mercury tilt switches, gravity switches and infra-red detectors or emitters. Several of the devices are sold commercially. The major disadvantage suffered by all of these devices is that they all require some form of instrumentation to be attached to the user. Since the device is being used by a disabled person an able bodied attendant is required to attach the instrumentation. This will limit the amount of independence that the device can infer. Nevertheless, this type of device is a major leap forward in improving the standard of living of the disabled.

A possible application in the realm of surgery has been suggested. During keyhole surgery a number of small incisions are made in a patient and an endoscope, manipulators and surgical tools are introduced. Too many pieces of equipment are used for the surgeon alone to control, he therefore has an assistant to manipulate the endoscope, and possibly some of the manipulators. Unless there is very good rapport between the surgeon and his assistant, the endoscope will often be misdirected. The surgeon's gaze direction could be used to automatically control the orientation of the endoscope. During surgery, the surgeon fixates on the monitor that displays the output of the endoscope, moving only his eyes to view different portions of the central region. Gross eye movements (i.e. fixating on an area of the screen outside of the central region) could be interpreted as a signal to the head pointing interface to redirect the endoscope.

A final example is the control of holographic displays for public spaces. A system has been suggested that can display a pair of images. One viewer is able to appreciate the holographic effect, the system monitors the viewer's head orientation and modifies the displayed data so as to maintain the three dimensional appearance.

Early uses of head pointing devices were in cognitive science research and were used to investigate eye movements in perceptual experiments. For example, to investigate the sequence of eye movements when a subject viewed a newspaper page. Since these were experimental devices, their user-friendliness was not an issue. In fact they were particularly un-user friendly: some required electrodes to be attached around the subject's eyes to measure the electrical activity in the eye muscles, some required special contact lenses which also measured the eye muscle's activity. In either case, the devices were particularly unpleasant for the subject to use, but tolerable in the experimental setting.

Video based head pointing devices are intended to implement a solution to the problem associated with earlier devices. Since they have no physical contact with the user, they require nothing to be attached to the user (or experimental subject), they are therefore easy to set up and use. In fact, the user should not be aware that he or she has started to use the device, except of course that the cursor follows his head or eye movements. The following sections describe the hardware and software required of the systems.

The Video Based Head Pointing Device: Hardware

The first requirement of any video processing application is to acquire the video data (Fig. 8.1). Fortunately, this problem is readily solved using either a framegrabber board contained within the host computer or one of the digital video cameras that plugs directly into the host's serial bus. There remains the question should colour or monochrome data be collected? It used to be the case that monochrome images were always

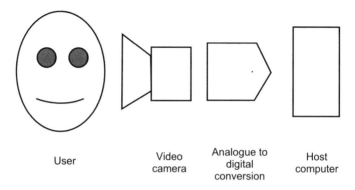

User   Video camera   Analogue to digital conversion   Host computer

Figure 8.1 Image acquisition hardware. The user is viewed by the video camera. The camera's output is digitised and stored on the host computer. When designing a system, many parameters are fixed e.g. the number of pixels in the image, the user must decide whether to capture colour or mono-chrome data and care must be taken when selecting the camera's lens, the field of view must be correct given the camera and the range of the user

collected due to the expense of colour data capture equipment and the time taken to process the colour data. These factors are not so important any more as colour capture devices are readily available and processors are now sufficiently powerful to process the extra data in an acceptable length of time. Colour information is usually collected because of the extra information it will yield. The advantages that this extra information provides more than outweighs the expense of processing it, indeed, some tasks may be performed more rapidly using a colour based algorithm than with an algorithm utilising monochrome data.

Whichever method of capturing data is chosen, the device must be able to deliver frames of video data with sufficient resolution to clearly identify image features that will allow the problem to be solved. For the head joystick, this means that features on the user's head (e.g. eyes, nose, mouth) must be unambiguously identified. For the eye mouse, it implies that the eyes must be located and the boundary of the iris and sclera identified with sufficient accuracy to estimate gaze. The frames must also be captured and processed at a rate high enough to enable the user's movements to be decoded. In practice, most image capture devices will be able to far exceed this requirement, it always turns out that the rate at which the data can be processed is the limiting factor in the overall processing rate.

The second problem to be addressed in considering the data acquisition problem, is the location and resolution of the camera to be used. The camera must be able to acquire images that are relevant to the problem being addressed, so the camera for the head joystick must acquire head images, and the eye mouse's camera must acquire images containing the eyes. The camera must be placed in close proximity to the monitor that is being viewed, the exact camera location will be discussed below.

Head Joystick Data Acquisition

The natural location for the camera in this application is adjacent to the user's monitor. Since the user will be looking at the monitor, a camera positioned there will always acquire the most relevant images. (It should be noted that the best images would be acquired by a camera located in the centre of the monitor. Whilst this cannot be realised directly, attempts have been made using mirrors to reflect images of the user onto a camera, but so far without success.)

Should the camera be located to one side, the top or bottom of the monitor? Cameras have often been sited on the top of the monitor, usually for no better reason than this provides a convenient surface for the camera. This results in the images of the user's head being less clear than they could be. As most people sit looking slightly downwards at the screen of their computers a camera sited on the top of the monitor will capture oblique images of the face and the eyes will be slightly obscured by the eyebrows. Siting the camera below the screen will sidestep this problem and result in improved images (the faces will still be slightly oblique, but matters cannot be improved beyond this state).

It was noted in Chapter 2 that the number of pixels in a digitised frame is dictated by national and international standards. Therefore the spatial resolution of the image can only be altered by changing the optics of the camera. Loosely this means that by using a lens with a shorter focal length we shall have wide-angle views in which the user's head is comparatively small, and using a lens with a longer focal length will deliver narrow-angle images in which the head is more closely framed. Whilst individual facial features will be more easily identifiable in the narrow-angle images, there will be less tolerance for the user's movement, even small movements could result in the head moving out of image. In practice, a compromise must be reached between the distance separating the user and the camera, the spatial resolution and the maximum allowed user movement.

Eye Mouse Data Acquisition

Similar requirements may be defined for data capture: the camera must deliver images in which the eyes are clearly visible, whilst allowing for the user's movement within the field of view. In this case, the requirements are more stringent in that the eyes must be imaged with a better resolution than any of the features in the head joystick images. This in turn restricts the angular size of the image since the number of pixels is fixed by the digitisation standards. The system's tolerance of any user movement is therefore much smaller.

An interesting solution to this difficulty has been suggested, which was to mount a miniature video camera on the frame of a pair of eyeglasses. The result was that the eye was imaged with more than satisfactory resolution and the eye never moved out of the camera's field of view. However, this solution violates the requirement that the device must be non-contact.

Summary

Acquiring optimum data for head pointing devices will always be a compromise between conflicting factors. The frame grabbing device will fix the number of pixels used to represent the image. A compromise must then be made between the smallest facial feature to be analysed, the distance of the subject from the camera, the camera's focal length (and hence its field of view) and the angular size of the image. The smallest feature to be analysed should be covered by as many pixels as practically possible, ten should be a reasonable number. The ratio of this number, to the horizontal image size (perhaps 780 pixels) will be equal to the ratio of the size of the smallest feature to the width of the imaged volume at the same range.

Greater resolution is required to image the facial features adequately. Lower resolution (a wider field of view) is required to give the user some tolerance for movement.

The Video Based Head Pointing Device: Software Requirements

At least four major functional requirements may be identified for the head pointing device's software. They are the same for both types of device. The requirements are all of equal importance.

The first requirement is for speed. Minimum processing rates in the order of 10 frames per second are required. Providing feedback to the user at this rate, or faster gives the illusion of continuous feedback and enables the user and the device to interact smoothly.

The second requirement is for accuracy. If the user looks at some point on the screen, the eye-mouse must move the cursor to that point. If the user inclines his head in some direction, the head-joystick must move the cursor in that direction.

The third requirement is for robustness: the software must function correctly for long periods. It must recover from error situations without the user being aware of the error. The system should also function correctly with a range of input data. Subjects with different skin colours, different amounts of facial hair, with and without glasses should all be able to use the system equally well.

The final requirement is ease of use. The system should require minimum calibration when a user begins to use it and should be as easy to use as the familiar mouse.

All of these requirements are of equal importance, there would be little value in having a head pointing device that gave feedback to its user at 10 frames per second, if that feedback was erroneous!

Possible Software Solutions

Although the functional requirements of the two types of system differ in some respects they share a significant similarity: both systems must isolate facial features, the eyes in one case and the eyes plus other features in the other. The operation of the two systems is also broadly similar, they must both go through an initialisation phase before they can be used in earnest. Both must also be able to simulate mouse clicks. The systems' functional requirements are so different that it is convenient to discuss them separately. The simulation of mouse clicks is common to both systems and will be discussed once.

Initialisation

The initialisation phase of operation will identify the presence of a face, thereby indicating that tracking is to commence. It will also determine a null direction – the state of the face when the user is focussed on the centre of the screen. The real world co-ordinates of the facial features will be sufficient to describe this state.

The presence of a face may be inferred by detecting differences between the current image and a reference image, by searching for large skin coloured areas or by searching for face shaped regions.

Probably the simplest method of recognising the presence of a face is by using the difference image. A reference image is captured when it is known that no user is present. For each succeeding image that is captured, a difference image is computed by subtracting it from the reference image. Regions that are significantly different are then investigated, looking for one region that is face shaped (approximately oval) or face coloured. When such a region is found it may be inferred that a user has sat in front of the monitor, ready to use the computer. At first it may be thought that facial colour is too variable to allow it to be used to identify faces. However, experimentation suggests that the largest component in the colour variation is due to differences in illumination. If this could be recognised and reduced it should be possible to identify a range of expected face colours. This can be achieved using normalised colour values, which are computed by dividing each colour component by the sum of colour components. Starting with a colour triplet [R, G, B] we compute normalised red and green components (the normalised blue is not needed as the normalised components sum to unity.) The observed range of the normalised values is sufficiently small to allow skin tone pixels to be recognised. Skin coloured regions would then be classified as face or non face according to their size. This is illustrated in Figure 8.2. Other colour representation methods can be used to achieve this goal, some yield a smaller range of skin colours.

Figure 8.2 Identifying the face using colour information. A colour image is split into red, green and blue bands. These may be separately thresholded and the results combined. The Results must be further processed to correctly identify the skin coloured regions. Deleting small or thin regions would accomplish this

The face may be identified by searching for skin coloured or face shaped regions without previously finding the regions of the image that are different to a reference image. For example, knowing the range of skin colours, we could simply search the current image for a contiguous set of pixels whose colours are within the allowed range, if this set is of the expected size, then a face has been identified.

The null direction is simply determined. In the case of the eye mouse, it is the position of the head and the eyes in their orbits when the user is looking at the centre of the screen. For the head joystick it is just the head position when the user is looking at the centre of the screen. How these states are recognised will be discussed below.

In some eye-mouse applications the user is also required to view targets placed strategically on the screen. This enables the system to recognise these specific directions of gaze and to interpolate the intervening directions.

Eye Mouse

To position the cursor, the eye mouse must find the face position and orientation and the location of the eyes in their orbits. The combination of these gives the user's direction of gaze. The intersection of this vector with the screen gives the focus of attention – the fixation point. The cursor must be moved to this point if it is onscreen, or to the nearest on-screen point if not.

Instantaneous eye locations will define the instantaneous fixation point. However, eye movement studies indicate that eyes are not scanned over a scene in a regular fashion. Rather the fixation point is moved very irregularly from one point of interest to another, often returning to previously visited fixation points. This is true even if the scene is something as highly structured as a page of text. If the cursor's location was updated instantaneously to reflect the fixation point, it would appear to move extremely erratically over the monitor. It is therefore necessary to deliver a smoothed estimate of the fixation point to the cursor update module. It might be sufficient to monitor the fixation points and disregard sudden deviations, retaining only those points that fit a trend of movements. Thus the cursor could be moved smoothly to its required destination.

A related problem is that of the user voluntarily looking away from the monitor. In less severe cases the system will manage to track the fixation point, but it will lie off-screen. In more severe cases, the eyes will be lost and tracking must be reinitialised.

Estimating the fixation point with sufficient accuracy to control modern software is probably the greatest problem for eye mouse systems. A typical screen may have a horizontal dimension of 0.3 m and display an image with a horizontal size of 800 pixels. If the user's eyes are 0.6 m from the screen, then each pixel will subtend an angle less than $0.2°$. Therefore the direction of gaze must be estimated to this degree of accuracy if the cursor is to be placed correctly. Naturally, the requirement can be eased according to the layout of the screen, but highly accurate measurements are still required.

The software functions by locating the face. It then locates the eyes within the face region of the image, and extracts sufficient information to estimate the direction of gaze vector. The pixels contributing to the face may be identified either using colour information or by considering the shape of the region they constitute.

Face Detection Using Colour Information

As described above and illustrated in Figure 8.2, the candidate face pixels may be selected by identifying those pixels that lie in the expected range of skin tones. Using the captured red, green and blue components will not give correct results as the variability of the data in this representation is much too large, changing the ambient illumination will change the perceived colours. However, the [R, G, B] data may be transformed into alternative representations in which the variation is much smaller, and skin colours are closely clustered, irrespective of the actual skin tone.

Several of the many colour models may be used for this purpose, the choice of which one is most applicable will be made according to the intended application and its users. The simplest modified colour model was described above, it is to use normalised red and green values that are computed by

$$r' = \frac{R}{R + G + B} \text{ and } g' = \frac{G}{R + G + B}$$

Some implementations add one to the denominator to prevent divide by zero problems. The normalised blue value is unnecessary, its value may be computed by subtracting the others from unity, including it will not therefore increase the amount of information. The model has a relatively large range for the r' and g' values of the skin tones. This will result in a relatively large number of false positives – pixels that are wrongly flagged as skin pixels which would have to be identified in a subsequent processing stage.

The hue, saturation and value and the Y, C_b, C_r models have also been used. Their disadvantage is that the captured data must be transformed into the new representation, adding another processing stage. Their advantage is that skin colours form a more compact cluster in these representations, thereby reducing the number of false positives.

The hue, saturation and value representation of a colour specifies the basic colour, the shade or depth of the colour and the brightness. Brightness is defined as the average of the red, green and blue components (an operation that gives incorrect weightings to the components). The colour co-ordinate is usually specified as an angle: red is defined as 0°, green as 120° and blue as 240°. The scale is discontinuous for shades near red. Saturation is defined as the depth of the colour. Because the colour co-ordinates are discontinuous, this representation is not often used in computations.

The Y, C_b, C_r colour model specifies the luminance (loosely the brightness) of a pixel and two colour difference values from which the three colour values may be computed. The components may be derived from the R, G, B values by

$$\begin{bmatrix} Y \\ C_b \\ C_r \end{bmatrix} = \begin{bmatrix} 16 \\ 128 \\ 128 \end{bmatrix} + \begin{bmatrix} 65.481 & 128.553 & 24.966 \\ -37.797 & -74.203 & 112.0 \\ 112.0 & -93.786 & -18.214 \end{bmatrix} \cdot \begin{bmatrix} R \\ G \\ B \end{bmatrix}$$

$$R, G, B \in [0 \ldots 1]$$

For processing colour data, the Y values are normally ignored, they encode the brightness variation of the data which is not normally of any use.

For any practical system, samples covering a large range of skin colour appearances are needed (different racial origins and different lighting conditions). The ranges of r′ and g′, S and V, or C_b and C_r spanning the samples can then be identified. It is usual to reduce the range of input colours before processing: digital colour is represented by 24 bit values, meaning that the colour space spans 256^3 colours. Even using two components results in a colour space of 256^2 values and performing a cluster analysis with this range of input is computationally expensive. The clustering is speeded up by reducing the number of distinct colours that must be represented. The skin coloured pixels are then aggregated into connected regions. The regions may be classified as face or not face according to their size: non-face regions are likely to be much smaller than the true face.

Face Detection Using Shape Information

Shapes are normally identified in monochrome images, no useful additional information is provided from the colour data. The face's outline is approximately elliptical and is usually oriented with the major axis closer to the vertical than the minor one. Tolerances can be placed on the maximum deviation of the major axis from the vertical, but this is not normally required. The process of recognising a face by its outline is illustrated in Figure 8.3.

The first step in determining the face's outline is to locate those points in the image that may be on the face boundary. This can be achieved by recognising that in most instances, the face is a different colour to the background. The colour difference manifests itself as a difference in the shade of grey between the face and non-face regions of the image.

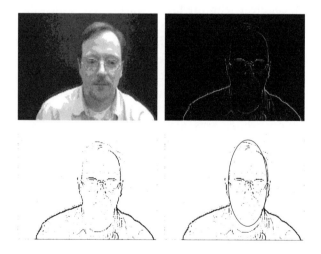

Figure 8.3 Identifying the face using shape information. The image has been enhanced by edge detection, thesholded and the pixels lying on a suitable sized ellipse have been identified

Differentiation of the image will enhance this difference and allow most, or even all of the boundary pixels to be identified, plus many other false boundary pixels. Many boundary enhancing operators have been defined, in practice, the Canny operator is used as its performance is superior in this case. (Edge detection is described in more detail in Appendix 2.)

The Canny operator is applied to the grey scale version of the face image. It first smoothes the image to reduce small scale, random fluctuations in brightness. It then differentiates the image in two directions: parallel to each side of the image. This can be thought of as being equivalent to measuring the two orthogonal components of a vector, in this case the vector corresponds to the direction and magnitude of maximum change of grey value in the image. The two differential images are combined, theoretically, they should be combined according to Pythagoras' rule, continuing the vector analogy, this is seen to be the equivalent of combining the vector components. In practice, it is sufficiently accurate to add the magnitudes of the components. The resulting image is then thresholded: values above some predetermined threshold are flagged as likely boundary points. These operations result in a binary image, that is, an image consisting of pixels that can take one of two values signifying that the pixel is a candidate boundary pixel or not.

In this image, we will observe contiguous boundary pixels that correspond to the face boundary. These sets of pixels are characteristically long and thin. We will also observe shorter, less regular segments of boundary pixels that correspond to other structures in the image: facial features or background structures. By grouping the longer segments we may gather evidence of the facial boundary. Grouping is achieved by extending the segments along the directions defined at their endpoints. If a second segment, collinear with the first is encountered, then the two are joined.

Other methods of finding the face boundary have been proposed, most notably the Hough transform. The Hough transform was first proposed to identify the presence of linear features in an image. It was later extended for all analytically defined shapes, and also for generalised shapes. In this case, a Hough transform is defined that will identify ellipses. (The Hough transform is described in more detail in Appendix 2.)

An ellipse whose axes are parallel to the image's x and y axes is described by the equation:

$$\frac{(x - x_\text{o})^2}{a^2} + \frac{(y - y_0)^2}{b^2} = 1$$

Where (x_0, y_0) are the co-ordinates of the centre of the ellipse and a and b are the lengths of its axes. The Hough transform defines an accumulator array that is used to gather evidence of all of the possible ellipses in an image. In this case, we would use a four dimensional array as the ellipse has four parameters. The image being processed would be edge enhanced as described above. All of the candidate boundary pixels are potentially on the boundary of the many ellipses that have suitable combinations of x_0, y_0, a and b.

The cells of the accumulator corresponding to all combinations of the parameters are incremented. Once all candidate boundary pixels have been processed, the cell in the accumulator that has most votes is deemed to represent the dominant ellipse present in the image, and the face has therefore been located.

This description is of course a gross simplification. First, we should introduce a fifth parameter to represent the ellipse's orientation. Second, a large ellipse is likely to receive many votes and will therefore be identified in preference to a smaller, but possibly more significant one. Third, the operation of computing the cells that should be incremented is extremely expensive, much effort has been directed towards finding efficient solutions to it. The number of cells in the accumulator is directly related to the number of parameters and their ranges and resolutions – too small a number and inaccurate ellipses will be found, too large a number and the ellipse finding will take a prohibitively long time to perform.

The Hough transform, which yields satisfactory results under ideal conditions, is not often used in this application as conditions are seldom ideal!

Feature Detection

Having found the face, the locations of the eyes and some other features must be determined. This will allow the head orientation to be computed, and the direction of gaze. This can be done in one of two ways, by searching for objects of known shape or by searching for dark regions. The shape of the face and expected locations of features are also used.

The face's anatomy provides extremely helpful clues as to the expected locations of features (Fig. 8.4). The face has a vertical line of reflective symmetry which will match the major axis of the ellipse that matched the face. In the top half of the face and equidistant from the axis of symmetry, the eyes will be found. The nose will be found in the centre of the face, more often the nostrils are found. And the mouth will be found in the lower portion of the face, orientated at right angles to the axis. This knowledge allows us to set up search regions for these features.

Therefore the eyes may be located by finding dark regions or circular shaped objects in the appropriate search region. The nose may be located by finding dark regions corresponding to the nostrils and the mouth by finding a linear structure in its search region. Having found these structures, each provides mutually supportive evidence for the identity of the others – the eyes' locations suggest a location for the mouth, which in turn suggests locations for the eyes.

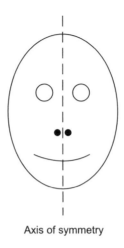

Axis of symmetry

Figure 8.4 Outline arrangement of facial features. Knowing this arrangement makes it simpler to identify facial features, typically, the eyes are identified first, this enables regions that should contain the nose and mouth to be guessed

Some features may also be identified directly from the original image data. For example, the irises are circular objects and can be detected using a Hough transform. Other features are identified by virtue of casting shadows, they are therefore defined by dark regions.

How Is the Fixation Point Estimated?

The fixation point is computed by intersecting the direction of gaze vector and the plane of the monitor screen. The direction of gaze vector is in turn defined by the location and orientation of the user's head and the position of the user's eyes in their orbits. These must be determined using the image data.

The head orientation is computed by taking the image co-ordinates of known features and projecting them back into the world to estimate their physical co-ordinates. A comparison of the instantaneous co-ordinates with those derived when the user was viewing the null point (during initialisation) will give the required estimate of head position and orientation.

The image co-ordinates are projected back into the real world by assuming that the camera system behaves as a simple pinhole camera. This implies that rays of light pass in a straight line through the camera's optical centre from object to image points. This is illustrated in Figure 8.5, which shows the image of a simple object (the arrows). Rays of light from the object pass through the optical centre of the camera system and hit the image plane (the camera's light sensitive plate) which is situated a distance f (the focal length) from the optical centre. Since the object and image are on opposite sides of the optical centre, one is an inverted

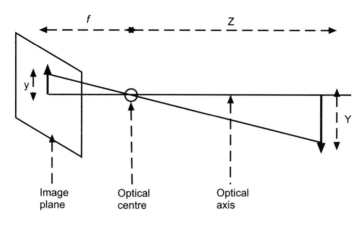

Figure 8.5 The pinhole camera model

version of the other. The object is situated at a distance Z from the optical centre, at co-ordinates (X, Y, Z). This distance is also known as the range.

Referring to Figure 8.5 we see that the object and the optical centre form a similar triangle with the optical centre and the image. We can then write:

$$\frac{y}{f} = \frac{Y}{Z}$$

This may be rearranged to give and expression from the Y co-ordinate of the object:

$$Y = \frac{Zy}{f}$$

There is an identical expression for the object's X co-ordinate.

The camera's focal length is known, but the range of the object cannot be determined. So absolute values of X and Y cannot be computed. The closest we may come to a knowledge of Z is its relation to its initial value: if the apparent size of the object increases, Z will have decreased. However, knowing scaled values of X and Y for sets of known features allows us to infer the head's orientation.

Having located three non-collinear points on the head (say the nose and eyes), the position (up to a magnification factor) and orientation of the head may be determined.

The second quantity to be determined is the position of the eyes within their orbits. This is the more important component in the direction of gaze, and whilst it is a difficult quantity to determine accurately using video based methods, it is possible.

When the user is looking straight ahead the areas of sclera (the white) that are visible between the iris and nose in each eye can be measured.

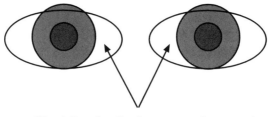

When in the null position these areas can be measured.
Deviations allow the eye orientation to be inferred.

Figure 8.6 Identifying the horizontal component to the direction of gaze by measuring the relative amounts of sclera visible in each eye

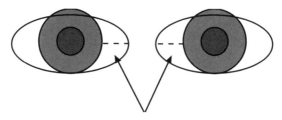

When in the null position these areas can be measured.
Deviations allow the eye orientation to be inferred.

Figure 8.7 Measuring the vertical component to the direction of gaze by measuring the amount of sclera visible beneath the iris' horizontal diameter

It is often thought that the areas should be equal, but this is not so, because one eye is usually dominant, that eye will be nearer the centre of the orbit than the other, Figure 8.6. By measuring deviations of these areas from the null, we may infer the horizontal movement of the eye and thus estimate the horizontal component of the direction of gaze. Similarly, if a line is drawn from the point on the iris border closest to the nose to the sclera's border we may infer the upward movement of the eye by comparing the areas of the sclera below the line, Figure 8.7. Obviously, such an approach can only be possible when the system has been calibrated with a carefully chosen set of targets. But once this process has been completed the eye-mouse can be reasonably accurate.

Update Rates

The eye-mouse must update the cursor position in "real time". Real-time represents a flexible amount of time, for video applications its shortest period is set by the video frame rate, 0.04 seconds or 25 updates per second. The longest period is approximately 0.1 seconds or 10 updates per second. This frequency represents an update rate that is perceived as continuous by humans. Most processors are not capable of performing large amounts of analysis within this target period. Some shortcuts are therefore required to increase the throughput of the processor.

The largest efficiency gain is to be made by tracking the target features rather than finding them afresh in each frame that is processed. Tracking a feature allows us to predict its likely location in a newly captured frame, given that we knew its movements in the previous frame. The feature's location is then verified and a model of its movements updated if necessary.

To model the movement of any object we assume that its motion can be described by Newtonian mechanics. Thus if an object is at a certain location at a certain time and is moving with constant velocity, we may integrate the velocity to predict the object's location at any future time. If the object also undergoes acceleration, we may include this. The object's location at any future time, $p(t + \Delta t)$, is therefore the sum of its current position, $p(t)$, the change in position due to its current velocity, $v(t)\Delta t$, and the change in position due to its acceleration $a(t)(\Delta t)^2/2$.

$$p(t + \Delta t) = p(t) + v(t)\Delta t + a(t) \frac{\Delta t^2}{2}$$

The predicted location can be used to define a small search window for finding the feature in question. Having located the feature, the difference between the actual and predicted locations can be used to correct the motion model for changes in velocity or acceleration. The instantaneous estimates of feature location, and hence the instantaneous estimate of gaze direction, will be corrupted by measurement noise and are therefore unlikely to be accurate. The errors in the measurements will have a zero mean: in the absence of movement, we may average a number of measurements to obtain the true value. If the feature is moving, then the current, noise corrupted, measurement may still be used to estimate the true feature location. Kalman filtering is one method of performing this operation.

The locations, velocity and acceleration are vector quantities. They may be measured as two-dimensional vectors based on image co-ordinates, or three-dimensional ones based on world co-ordinates, scaled to a fixed Z value. Either representation is valid.

Conclusion

The eye-mouse has appeared in various guises, using additional hardware worn by the user, using infra-red illumination and, most difficult of all, using purely video based methods. Systems that require the user to wear additional hardware, and systems using IR illumination are in use and have proved to be satisfactory.

The same cannot be said for current video based systems. They have proved to be difficult to use because of the accuracy requirement: the data does not allow sufficiently accurate estimates of direction of gaze to be made, the cursor's position cannot in turn be controlled with sufficient accuracy to allow the systems to be used reliably.

Rather than dismiss this approach to solving a real problem. Two modifications have been suggested. First, a research group at IBM suggested that the video based eye-mouse should be used to control the gross movement of the cursor and a normal mouse be used to provide fine control. Second, the video based system should be used to control the cursor as a joystick, not a mouse.

Head Joystick

The requirements of the head joystick are less stringent because of its intended function. The system must capture images of the user and move the onscreen cursor in the direction defined by the user's head orientation. Movement of the cursor will continue until the user returns his head to the null position. Operation of the head joystick is similar to the head-mouse in that it is initialised similarly, some features on the head are identified and their positions compared with their null co-ordinates. The cursor is moved according to any change in the features' locations.

During execution, the head-joystick performs a very similar task to the head-mouse. The user's head is identified, facial features are located on the head and their image co-ordinates projected back into world co-ordinates. Head orientation is thereby determined and the cursor is moved accordingly. The steps involved are the same as described above.

Programming the head-joystick is simpler as there is less of a demand for accuracy. Consequently, users of the head joystick find it less demanding to use as they do not have to fixate carefully on the screen for long periods of time. The system compensates for its inaccuracies by providing immediate feedback: if the cursor is not quite moving in the correct direction, the user is able to issue corrective instructions.

Mouse Clicks

Simulation of mouse clicks can vary according to the intended users of the system. Some systems used by the disabled use suck and puff switches, the user operates a pressure switch by sucking or blowing through a tube. The pressure switch is interfaced to the mouse port. The IBM eye-mouse (known as "Blue Eyes") is used in conjunction with a normal mouse, the eye-mouse is used to perform gross cursor movements, the desktop mouse provides fine control plus the button functions. The video based mouse or joystick must interpret suitable facial gestures as mouse clicks.

Since most desktop computers have a mouse with two buttons, it is natural to require a gesture that can be made in left-handed or right-handed versions to mimic the mouse button clicks. Such a gesture could be a wink or either eye, or a half smile with either half of the mouth. The video based mouse or joystick must, in addition to its cursor positioning function, monitor the face for these gestures. This can only be done with sufficient speed if the positions of the features are tracked from frame to frame through the video sequence. The software is then able to search the eye region for pixels the of the iris colour or the mouth region to identify changes in shape from the relaxed shape.

In the case of the eye gesture, if sufficient iris pixels are found, it may be assumed that the eye is open and no action needs be taken. If fewer than a predetermined number of pixels are located, the eye is either closed, closing or opening and a wink or a blink is in progress. It has been shown that a wink is significantly longer than a blink, a blink will not be observed in more than one frame, assuming frame rates of about 10 per second. Therefore, if a closed eye event is observed in more than one consecutive frame, a wink is in progress and the appropriate action should be performed. Both eyes must be monitored, as either can be used to simulate a single mouse click. If both eyes a winked simultaneously, we may infer a double mouse click.

For the mouth gesture, we may compare the current mouth outline against a template. If there is a significant difference between the template and the pattern in the left, right or both halves, then a left, right or double click may be inferred. The matching process must allow for rotations of the outline.

Conclusions

The video based mouse or joystick has received considerable interest from the research community over the recent years. Significant progress has been made in developing devices that have given disabled users a high degree of independence. Much work remains to be done in developing low cost devices that may be used with no additional hardware and require minimal setting up. It is also extremely important that devices such as these are developed and assessed in conjunction with the intended users.

This chapter has described the image capture mechanisms and one method of processing the data to regain direction of gaze. Many other methods of performing this computation have been proposed, most notably the use of artificial neural networks (ANNs). In this approach, a network is trained to associate a direction of gaze with a particular type of image. Provided that the set of images used to train the network is appropriately chosen to contain suitable numbers of examples and counter examples, the approach ought to be successful. No full scale working version has yet been deployed.

Bibliography

Printed Material

Drew R, Pettitt S, Blenkhorn P, Evans DG (1998) "A Head Operated 'Joystick' Using Infrared", *Computers and Assistive Technology ICCHP '98, Proc XV IFIP World Computer Congress*, Edwards ADN, Arato A, Zagler WL (eds), Österreichische Computer Gesellschaft,

Gee AH, Cipolla R (1998) "Tracking faces", in *Computer Vision for Human-Machine Interaction*, Cipolla R, Pentland A (eds), Cambridge University Press, Cambridge.

Ivins J (1992) "A prototype Eye-Tracking Human-Computer Interface for Estimating the Direction-of-Gaze of Disabled Users", MSc dissertation, Department of Computation, UMIST.

Gunn SR, Nixon MS (1996) "Snake head boundary extraction using local and global energy minimisation". *Proc. International Conference on Pattern Recognition ICPR '96*, volume B, pp. 581–5.

McKenna SJ, Gong S, Raja Y (1998) "Modelling Facial Colour and Identity with Gaussian Mixtures" *Pattern Recognition* 31:1883–92.

Rowley HA, Baluja S, Kanade T, (1995) "Human Face Detection in Visual Scenes", *CMU Technical Report CMU-CS-95–158R*, School of Computer Science, Carnegie Mellon University.

Sirohey SA (1993) "Human face segmentation and identification", Computer Vision Lab Technical Report CS-TR-3176, University of Maryland.

Stroud JM (1956) "The fine structure of psychological time". In Quastler H (ed.) *Information Theory in Psychology*, Freepress, Glencoe Ill.

Internet Resources

Commercial Eye-Mouse Type Devices:

Organisation http://www.orin.com/access/
Organisation http://www.prentrom.com/access/hm2000.html
LC Technologies: http://www.lctinc.com/
Organisation http://www.madenta.com/
Organisation http://www.smi.de/home/index.html
Multimo: http://atwww.hhi.de:80/~blick/

Research Groups

Blue Eyes: http://www.almaden.ibm.com/cs/blueeyes/

9 Gesture Recognition

Introduction

Gesture recognition is the process of interpreting by computer any gestures made by a user. A computer system that uses gestures as an input mode may provide a more natural human-computer interface than is currently available. In office environments it could allow people to select objects or text for editing by pointing directly at the text or object. Graphical objects could be manipulated more easily by gesture than by mouse: an object could be selected by pointing at it, it could be rotated by a hand rotation, it could be resized by expansion or shrinking gestures. Interactive computer games would be enhanced if the computer could "understand" the players' hand gestures. Gesture based interfaces would also have applications in the home, an appliance could be selected or activated by pointing at it, a specific repertoire of gestures would then be available for controlling it. A television's channels could be changed by holding up fingers to indicate the required channel number, or the viewer could point forwards or backwards to incrementally change channels. Similarly, a simple repertoire of gestures could be defined for controlling other appliances.

In Chapter 9 we shall examine some sample gesture interfaces that have been suggested and implemented by various research groups. By examining these, we shall discover the properties that are required of a gesture based computer. These requirements will be summarised and then examined in detail. The systems described in this chapter are concerned with gestures made with the hand and fingers. The following chapter will describe systems that attempt to understand movements of the whole body.

Example systems

This section will examine three proposed gesture based systems: one to control home appliances, one to replace the mouse in desktop computing systems and one to recognise gestures relating to sign language. At the end of the section, common properties of the systems will be identified, this will allow us to derive requirements for general purpose gesture interfaces.

TV Remote Control

Researchers at Mitsubishi's laboratories in Cambridge developed a gesture based system that replaced the television remote control. Their justification of this choice of system was the result of a survey in which Americans were asked what "high tech" gadget had most improved their quality of life. The top two responses were the microwave oven and the television remote control. The researchers set out to improve the remote control by replacing it with a gesture or a voice based system. They dismissed voice input as being too tiring in some modes of operation (channel surfing or incrementally adjusting controls) and too difficult to realise given the ambient noise that would be present.

The researchers required a gesture that could be easily made (it had to be simple and non tiring) and easily recognised by their control systems (which would imply rapid processing and error free operation). They selected holding the hand up with the palm facing the television. When the system observed this gesture (the trigger gesture), it would enter its control mode and moving the hand would select the various controls and alter their levels.

The open hand gesture was located in each image captured by the input device by correlating the input image with a template – a small image of an archetype open hand. In their demonstration system, the trigger gesture had to be maintained for approximately half a second before being recognised. Hand location information was used to optimise hand tracking, hand locations were computed at a rate of 5 Hz and the television was accurately controlled.

Figure 9.1 illustrates schematically the arrangement of the remote control system and Figure 9.2 illustrates typical feedback provided by the system: buttons and the slider controls are shown, together with a representation of the user's hand position and the hot-spot that is used as the control point (when the hotspot itself overlies one of the controls, the control is activated).

The Gesture Computer

The Gesture Computer was developed by researchers at Siemens in Munich. Originally the project was intended to develop general purpose

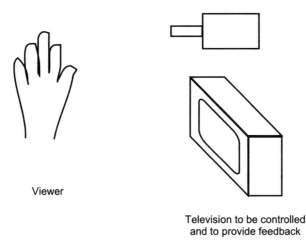

Monitoring camera

Viewer

Television to be controlled
and to provide feedback

Figure 9.1 Schematic layout of Mitsubishi's television gesture remote control

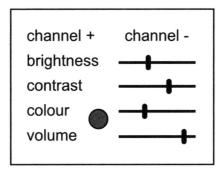

Figure 9.2 The on-screen feedback provided by Mitsubishi's system

gesture mediated communication systems. These would find applications in the office, in advertising, in harsh or dirty environments and in teleconferencing. In this section we shall examine their office based systems.

There are characteristic operations that are performed when using a workstation in an office. When editing or writing text, a cursor must be positioned in a document, text may be selected and blocks of text may be moved or deleted. To achieve these operations, a cursor is moved using a mouse and positioned by clicking a mouse button. Text is selected or moved by clicking and dragging. Similarly, when designing graphical objects, elements may be drawn, selected, edited or removed. The view of the object may be altered by moving the viewpoint towards or away from the object, or around the object. The usual mouse and button operations are to be replaced by a vocabulary of gestures, pointing type movements would control the positioning of the cursor and selecting of objects. Other gestures would replace the deleting or moving commands.

In order to recognise these gestures, the Gesture Computer had to identify the hands, the fingers and the positions of each of the fingers. The target hand was isolated from the background using colour information. The normalised red and blue values were computed and used to construct a colour histogram for small blocks of pixels. Blocks whose histograms closely resembled the histogram of skin colours were labelled as skin, and assumed to belong to the hand. Due to the scene characteristics, it is unlikely that there will be a significant number of skin coloured blocks outside of the hand region. From these blocks, the hand centre and orientation were computed, a window was drawn around the hand to define a search region for the following frame. Temporally smoothed estimates of hand position and orientation were derived to reduce the variation due to image noise. The relative distance between the hand and the camera was estimated by comparing the current hand size to the hand size when the system was initialised. In this way the system was able to estimate the hand's orientation and position in space. Figure 9.3 summarises the hand identification process.

Recovering the finger configurations would seem to be a complex problem, as the fingers collectively have 19 degrees of freedom. Figure 9.4 illustrates the rotational degrees of freedom of one finger. However, the movements of the fingers are very constrained and it is possible to estimate the joint angles if the position of the fingertip is known. This approach was taken by the researchers at Siemens. They created a lookup table that related joint angles to fingertip position by positioning the fingers at known joint angles and measuring the fingertip positions. The fingertips' positions relative to the palm of the hand were found in the video data, and the closest match in the lookup table determined the joint angles.

The completed system was capable of processing ten frames of data per second. Hand position and orientation was determined accurately, the finger configurations were not found so reliably. However, if finger configurations were found, then matching against known gestures could be attempted. The system was capable of recognising a rudimentary set of gestures.

Interpreting Sign Language

Researchers at Michigan State University have developed a system that attempts to recognise the gestures made when speaking using sign language. In their work, they selected a subset of American Sign Language: twenty-eight different signs made using one hand. The signs are made up of different finger configurations and movements of the hand. The finger configurations, and the start and end points of the movement all

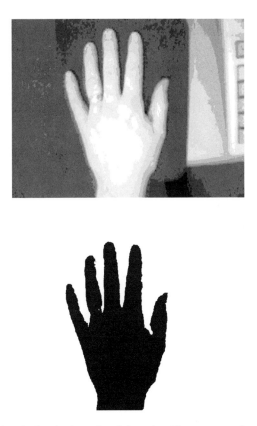

Figure 9.3 Identifying the hand using colour information. The same set of operations has been performed as for detecting the face using this method

contribute to the gesture's meaning. They must therefore all be determined from the video sequence.

The system first isolated the hand in the video sequence. The hand region was then resampled to a standard size and represented as a column matrix (stacked). The stacked hand regions in each image from the sequence were aggregated into a single (large) column matrix. This data structure captured the spatial and temporal information of the gesture. It was compared against the data derived from known gestures. The completed system was able to recognise gestures with a success rate of 93%. However, the processing time was impractically long – 54 seconds per image.

Common Themes

The most obvious requirement of these systems is to capture appropriate colour information of the scene. The resolution of the data must be correct for the data being captured: the field of view must encompass

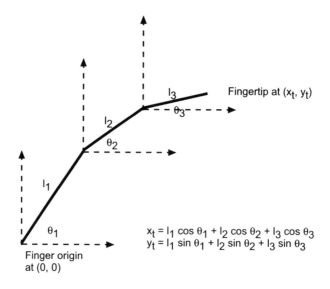

Figure 9.4 Three degrees of freedom of a finger. The finger can also rotate in and out of the plane about its base. Each finger therefore has four degrees of freedom, and the thumb has three

the whole volume of the scene in which the gestures are likely to occur. For a workstation system, this would be the volume situated between the user and the workstation screen. The image data must have a resolution capable of resolving the objects of interest, i.e. the fingers.

The second common theme is the ability to recognise gestures. We must first define what a gesture is. A simple definition is that a gesture is a recognisable configuration of the user's fingers. Thus, holding the hand upright with the fingers extended and touching would mean "stop". Making a circle with the thumb and forefinger and extending the other fingers would mean "OK", and so on. This type of gesture may be termed a "static gesture" since it is composed of a static configuration of the fingers.

We may extend the vocabulary of gestures by including movement, that is viewing a gesture as a spatiotemporal event. In this definition, the fingers are allowed to move between fixed configurations. The combination of movement or movements and configurations constitutes the gesture. Beckoning or directing typify these gestures.

It is of interest to note that none of these systems attempts to recognise gestures made using the arms, instead of or in addition to the hands. This is due to the fact that the arms will add little to the vocabulary of the hands and fingers. And also, practically, if the system is to capture images of the arms and the fingers, there would be too much data to be processed within a reasonable time.

Requirements

Colour images provide additional information that can be useful for identifying hands and fingers in video sequences. That is not to say that hands and fingers cannot be identified in monochrome images. Indeed, using colour images requires three times as much data to be processed and there will be no benefit unless significantly faster and more reliable algorithms can be derived to process this information.

The resolution of the data must be compatible with the type of gesture to be recognised. The image area must span the gesturing volume with a resolution appropriate to the objects being viewed. For an office interface, the image area would correspond to the user's desk and the resolution to the smallest text being processed. For interpreting sign language, the image area would correspond to the volume immediately in front of the signer's head and torso, the resolution must be capable of visualising the signer's fingers.

The position of the camera must also be considered carefully. An office system would have the camera viewing the workspace, this could be paper on the user's desk, or it could be the workstation screen. The camera could therefore be positioned vertically above the user, or immediately behind him. For reading sign language, the signer would be seated in front of the camera.

As with other multimedia communication systems, these systems must deliver a response at a rate that is compatible with the rate at which the user is communicating with them and at a rate compatible with the user's ability to perceive it – too fast and information will be lost, too slow and the data will appear to be episodic. In practice, a response time of some 100 ms is appropriate. Within this time, the system must capture an image, extract the required information from it, identify the configuration of the fingers and hand, recognise the configuration state and provide feedback to the user.

Gestures may be composed of single hand configurations, or multiple configurations and the transition or transitions between them. The gesture systems must be able to identify the instantaneous hand and finger configurations and the transitions between them. The combined information must be recognised as a gesture. At this moment, no systems have been developed that are capable of fulfilling this requirement.

Identifying and Describing Hands and Fingers in Video Sequences

Gestures may be identified and represented using methods that range in complexity and reliability. Some methods represent gestures or limbs using information derived directly from the pixel data. These methods tend to be unsophisticated and often less reliable than other alternatives. At the other extreme, some methods use pixel data to modify the parameters of a statistical model of the object being sought. The model can also be used to guide the information extraction. Since much information has been used to generate the statistical model, these methods tend to be more reliable, if less sensitive to the specific data being processed. Three methods of segmenting the video data will be described that span the range from simple to sophisticated techniques.

Orientation Histograms

The orientation histogram is a method of computing the differences between an image of a sample gesture and images of known gestures, a small difference would suggest that the sample and known images were similar. A simplistic approach to computing the difference between the sample and known gestures would be to sum the differences between the equivalent pixels in the pair of images. However, this technique is too sensitive to other causes of image differences, for example changes in illumination or a difference between the hand locations in the two images. Instead we need a difference measure that is insensitive to the hand's location within the image and to changes in illumination. One way of achieving this is to form a histogram of the locally dominant orientations.

Local orientation may be computed by convolving the image with a large number of differently oriented filters. Conceptually, these are similar to the edge detecting filters described in Appendix 2, but rather than compute edge strength in two orthogonal directions, edge magnitudes are estimated in as many as eight or twelve orientations. The filter giving the maximum response determines the local orientation. The histogram of the local orientations over the whole image is computed and plotted on a polar diagram: radial values indicate the frequencies of edge orientation occurrence, and angle maps to orientation, Figure 9.5. The envelope of the histogram is supposed to be characteristic of the gesture.

The authors of this method suggest that this provides a simple, quick method of extracting a description of a gesture. The method works well most of the time, it is most accurate when the images from which prototype histograms were derived have the same level of illumination as the current images. Some sets of gestures are confused, as are rotated gestures. Further, the hand must be the dominant object in the image, otherwise the local edge information will be derived from irrelevant data.

Colour Based Methods

We have seen previously that faces may be located in video data by looking for skin coloured pixels. The same techniques may be applied to

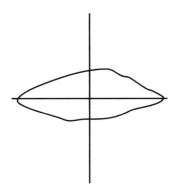

Figure 9.5 A polar plot of an edge orientation histogram

locating the hands and fingers for gesture recognising systems. One working system compares the known distribution of skin colours against the distribution of colours in small regions of the image.

The image is divided into small regions. The size of the regions may be dynamically altered to reflect the processing load; smaller regions and hence a more accurate segmentation are used when the resources are available, otherwise, time is saved by using larger regions. The colour values of pixels in the region are normalised, as before. Two colour values per pixel are derived according to

$$r' = \frac{R}{R\ +\ G\ +\ B\ +\ 1} \text{ and } b' = \frac{B}{R\ +\ G\ +\ B\ +\ 1}$$

Adding one to the denominator ensures that finite values are computed for black regions (where the R, G and B values are zero). The colour values are also quantised to a smaller range of values: d values rather than the more normal 256. The colour histogram is therefore a d by d array of frequency values.

The known skin histogram ($H^p(i,j)$) is compared against each of the histograms computed from the regions using a similarity measure:

$$M_{p,q} = \frac{\sum_{i,j} \min(H^p(i,j), H^q(i,j))}{\sum_{i,j} H^p(i,j)}$$

Values of M greater than 0.9 indicate a good match between the histograms, the patch is therefore from a skin region. This high threshold value means that some skin regions will be erroneously classified as non-skin. Reducing the value of the threshold would result in these blocks being correctly labelled, but would also result in non-skin blocks being labelled as skin regions. The authors of the technique decided that it was more important to avoid misclassifying non-skin blocks.

The initial colour histogram was derived in one of two ways. It may be given default values derived from images of a large number of hands captured under the same conditions as when the system was being used. These values should be dynamically modified to more accurately reflect the specific hand being tracked. Alternatively, the histogram may be initialised during a system initialisation phase. An image would be captured of the hand in a standard configuration: palm down on the desk, directly below the camera, with the fingers separated, for example. The hand would be identified in this image and the colour histogram could be derived for this specific user.

Having completed the segmentation, a low resolution skin image is available for further processing. Although this is a simple technique, it has been shown to be reliable and fast.

Flexible Templates

Flexible templates were defined as a method of representing the variation in the shape of a natural structure. The impetus for their development came from the requirement to derive a compact representation of simple objects whose normal appearances varied considerably. It is a statistical technique that depends on identifying an average shape and the usual modes of variation.

The template is constructed from samples of the shape to be represented. For a gesture recognition system, this means that we must obtain samples of all of the gestures to be recognised by the system. The set of samples must reflect the ranges of gestures and their frequencies. Although the sample gestures are made with the hands in a standardised position and configuration, perfect positioning and alignment cannot be achieved. The hand images are therefore normalised to reduce this variation before any further processing. The normalisation involves rotating and scaling the image to bring the hand to a standard orientation and size. The remaining variation in the data is due to the differences in finger configurations when making the gesture. From each sample we extract the information to be used to build the template: a set of points defining the outline of the hand, Figure 9.6. The points must be identified consistently in each sample The average locations and the covariances of the locations of the samples' points are computed. The covariance matrix records the variation in the values of each points co-ordinates and the variation in one co-ordinate as a consequence of variations in a second. If we had n points around the outline of a hand, the average vector would have $2n$ elements (two co-ordinates per point) and the covariance matrix will have $2n \times 2n$ elements. If the points were plotted on a graph (with $2n$) axes, they would form an elongated cloud.

A principal component analysis of the covariance is then performed. This effectively rotates the axes of the sample space such that most of

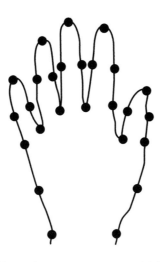

Figure 9.6 Generation of a flexible template to represent gestures. It is important that the set of control points is indicated consistently in all of the hand images. Otherwise the control points will capture information relating to the gesture and the distribution of control points

the data's variation lies along one axis – the first principal component, most of the remaining variation lies along a second axis – the second principal component and so on. The data can be equivalently represented by using all of the axes defined by the principal component analysis. We may also approximately represent the original information using the first few components. The accuracy of the representation is dictated by the number of components that are used. It transpires that a hand outline can be represented with sufficient accuracy for recognition with nine coefficients.

In use, the outline of a hand would be derived, the required number of points located and projected onto the nine principal component axes. The projected values will allow the gesture to be recognised.

Summary

Three methods of describing the hands and fingers have been described. All are successful provided that some preconditions are met. For example, the orientation histogram technique requires that the hand is the largest object in the image and that gestures are made with consistent orientations. If these requirements are met, then the system can recognise simple gestures.

The three methods also illustrate different methods of representing the hands and fingers. One system derived data characteristic of the gesture from the images. This data is then compared against equivalent data derived from prototype gestures. The other systems illustrate the two alternative methods of representing a region in an image: by identifying the pixels constituting the region, or the pixels forming the boundary of the regions. Neither method provides completely correct results: the region based method will occasionally loose blocks of the hand, and the boundary based method will deliver a boundary that sometimes deviates from the true boundary. Nevertheless, the results are sufficiently accurate to allow gesture recognition to take place.

Tracking Hands and Fingers in Video Sequences

Tracking of features may occur in one of two ways. If the feature description method is simple and quickly executed, then it may be performed on each image that is captured. Such a method would not require any information from a previous image to guide processing of the current one and thereby increase the processing rate to an acceptable level. Simple algorithms such as orientation histograms or colour based segmentation may achieve real-time performance in this way, but will still benefit from using guiding information. For example, it may be assumed that the hand does not move significantly in the time between capturing images. The location of the hand in one image will therefore be similar to the hand location in the next one and can be used to suggest a search area in the second image.

Other algorithms are too complex to process the entire image at the target processing rates. In these cases, information from the previous frame or frames must be used to reduce the amount of processing required to analyse the current frame. These methods will follow the principle of the cycle of perception, introduced in chapter five, in which the results of processing one frame are used to guide the capture and focus the processing of the next frame.

In the previous chapter, the future locations of facial features were predicted using a motion model that assumed the features moved as inertial objects (i.e. following Newton's laws of motion). The locations were predicted by adding the integrated acceleration and velocity to the feature's current position. This method could be applied to predicting the location of the hand as a whole, but is inappropriate for predicting the locations of the fingers as they are too small and featureless to allow the positions of the different fingers to be determined reliably. (To overcome the similarity problem, one research group suggested that their subjects should wear multicoloured gloves, each digit was uniquely coloured.) In most applications prediction is restricted to identifying a search window centred on the current hand location. The hand is sought in this window in the following image.

One benefit conferred by predictive tracking was the generation of a smooth locus for the feature's movement, this was due to the fact that the motion model imposed on the feature assumed smooth movement.

Since we are not able to use a motion model, and have to locate the features in each image with little help from previous images, the feature's loci may be irregular. The irregularities may be smoothed by maintaining a running average of the locations: the smoothed location is computed as a weighted sum of the current estimated location and the current location as determined from the image:

$$\hat{r}_t = (1 - \alpha)\hat{r}_{t-1} + \alpha r_t$$

The parameter α is used to control the contribution of the image data to the smoothed hand position. Making α smaller will result in the hand position being derived mainly from the predicted positions. The locus will be smooth, but probably inaccurate. At the other extreme, setting α to 1 will result in the smoothed estimate being identical to the measured position. Consequently, the locus will be accurate, but irregular.

Representing Gestures

A range of gesture representations exist, ranging from simple techniques that represent the gesture data with little processing of the pixel data to more complex methods that attempt to explicitly model the state of the hand and fingers. Representing a gesture using raw data may seem an attractive option since it requires little processing of the data, however, this is also the cause of the major problem associated with this type of method: it is sensitive to other factors that influence the pixel values, not just the gestures themselves. Even a simple change in illumination will have a misleading affect on the representation.

Techniques that extract information from the image to build an abstract representation of the gesture are less influenced by non-gestural factors. For example, a gesture recognition system using the flexible template technique will not be influenced by changes in the scene's illumination – these changes may alter the details of the boundary that is generated, but this error will be absorbed by the representation and recognition schemes.

If we are attempting to represent a gesture we ought to record the position of the hand and all nineteen of the joint angles, since it is this information that constitutes the gesture. Determining this information from a two dimensional image of the hand is a difficult problem, in fact it is not soluble for many finger configurations. The GestureComputer described above suggested a partial solution in which it was assumed that the finger joints did not move independently, therefore their angles could be postulated from the palm and fingertip locations. However, the joint angles could not be determined accurately, nor uniquely by this method. It is probably impossible to accurately determine joint angles from an image of the hand; because of the limited resolution of the image, and the fact that it is a two-dimensional representation of the three-dimensional scene.

Is it necessary to determine joint angles? When one person makes a gesture to the other, is the gesture made and comprehended with any reference to joint angles? Probably not, we make gestures by curling the fingers to a greater or lesser degree, by separating or aligning fingers, and by moving them. This would suggest that gestures ought to be interpreted by symbolically representing the amount of curvature of each finger: is it straight, tightly curved into a fist or loosely curved. This analysis could be extended by recording the related behaviour of the fingers, for example the third and fourth fingers do not move independently. No system has yet been implemented using this technique. Perhaps the systems that come closest are those that represent gestures by recording the outline of the hand as it makes them, flexible template based systems for example.

Recognising Gestures

Recognition of a gesture is achieved by matching the sample gesture against a set of labelled gestures. The method used to perform the matching is dictated by the representation of the gesture. Methods of performing the recognition have been suggested above, where different representation techniques were discussed.

Essentially, all of the techniques measure the difference between a pattern derived from the gesture to be recognised and the patterns derived from known gestures, as stored in the database. The gesture is given the label of the sample pattern for which this difference is the smallest:

$$s \in C_I \text{ if } D(s_I,s) < D(s_I,s_j) \ \forall \ i \neq j$$

The pattern, s, may be a polar representation of an orientation histogram, it may be the values of the first six principal components of an object's outline, or any other description of the gesture. Many variations of the distance function have been proposed, ranging from measures using Pythagoras' theorem, probabilistic measures to symbolic manipulations.

It is important that the gesture database is representative of the range of gestures and users that will use the system. If not, the system will fail to recognise the missing gestures, or recognise them incorrectly.

Summary and Conclusions

This chapter has described gesture mediated human computer interfaces. In these, the usual communication channels are augmented with gestures, the computer is given the ability to recognise the gestures and associate with them an action to be performed.

Sample gesture based systems were examined. A pragmatic definition of a gesture was then derived: a gesture is a spatiotemporal event, it is composed of the movement of fingers between different configurations. Whilst gestures may be made with the arms, this class of gesture is not so interesting as it is much more limited in its vocabulary.

Based on this definition, we may design systems that will respond to gestures. Such a system must first isolate the hands and fingers in each frame of a video sequence. From this information the configuration of the fingers may be estimated. Processing of the video sequence will yield a sequence of finger states interspersed with transitions. This is similar to the process of deriving a sequence of phonemes when attempting to recognise speech from an audio signal, except that the diphones are not of any interest when recognising speech, the transitions between hand configurations may be important for gesture understanding. Sequences of finger states may then be grouped into meaningful gestures; gestures will be composed of one or more states. Methods of identifying and tracking hands and fingers were then examined. Finally, methods of recognising gestures were described.

At present, gesture based computers are restricted to research laboratories. Some gesture mediated systems have been released, we could argue that a touchscreen may fulfil some of the requirements of office systems. Datagloves have been available for some time. These are gloves that include strain gauges that measure the angles of the finger joints and transmit them to a host computer. They are, however very restrictive for the user.

In the near future, gesture computers are likely to be released for general use. Office based systems are likely to be available first, followed by systems intended for use in dirty or hazardous environments where a keyboard is impractical.

Bibliography

Printed Material

Ahmad S (1994) "A usable real-time 3D hand tracker", *Proc IEEE 28th Asilomar Conference on Signals, Systems and Computer.*

Ahmad T, Taylor CJ, Lantinis A, Cootes TF (1995), "Recognising hand gestures using statistical shape models", *Proc 6th British Machine Vision Conference*, Birmingham.

Cipolla R, Pentland A (1998) (eds) Computer Vision for Human-Machine Interaction, CUP, Cambridge.

Freeman WT, Roth M (1995) "Orientation histograms for hand gesture recognition", IEEE International Workshop on Automatic Face and Gesture Recognition, Zurich.

Freeman WT, Weissman CD (1995) "Television control by hand gestures", IEEE International Workshop on Automatic Face and Gesture Recognition, Zurich.

Maggioni C, Kämmerer B (1998) "GestureComputer – history, design and applications", in *Computer Vision for Human-Machine Interaction*, Cipolla R, Pentland A (eds), CUP, Cambridge.

Weng JJ, Chu Y (1998) "Recognition of hand signs from complex backgrounds", in *Computer Vision for Human-Machine Interaction*, Cipolla R, Pentland A (eds), CUP, Cambridge.

Internet Resources

Gesture Recognition Home Page: http://www.cybernet.com/~ccohen/gesture.html

WT Freeman at Mitsubishi Labs, Cambridge, Massachusetts: http://www.merl.com/people/freeman/

VISLab Fingermouse at University of Illinois at Chicago: http://vislab.eecs.uic.edu/PROJECT/Fmouse/Fmouse.homepage.html

10 Motion Following and Interpretation

Introduction

Previous chapters have dealt with multimedia systems that are very definitely fixed in the laboratory or home: we have discussed systems that have been essentially novel methods of interacting with the computer. Chapter 10 takes multimedia systems out of that context and examines how we may develop multimedia systems able to comprehend unrestricted movement.

Motion following and interpretation systems fall into one of two categories. One category is formed of those systems that capture sequences of images of a scene and attempt to derive a description of the activity occurring in the scene. We may decide, for example, to make security cameras more intelligent by introducing software that is capable of describing the activities happening in a shopping centre, or a car park. The system would be provided with descriptions of the types of activities it would expect to see, and would be programmed to give the appropriate responses. As an example, a system monitoring a car park would expect to see drivers and their passengers leaving or returning to their vehicles. We would expect them to leave the car park by the closest exit and to return directly to the vehicle. Any deviation from this path might be viewed as suspicious, or at least worthy of further investigation: the motorist may have forgotten the car's location, Figure 10.1.

The second category is an extension of the provision of multimedia interactivity. In this category of system we dispense entirely with the keyboard and mouse, and rely exclusively on sound and visual input and output. The users of these systems are permitted to make any gestures and are free to locate themselves anywhere in the scene. The system is expected to interpret those gestures in the context of the task that is to be performed. The system will provide feedback in a multimedia manner, that is an anthropomorphic representation of the system is used to project the system's understanding of and response to any input.

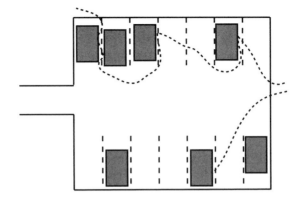

Figure 10.1 Normal (lower) and suspicious (upper) behaviour of people walking through a car park

This chapter will deal with the methods used to implement these systems: that is, how are activity understanding systems created, and how should we extract and recognise unrestricted gestural and sound input. Chapter 11 is concerned with providing visual feedback.

Activity Understanding Systems

All activity understanding systems will be composed of the same or similar components and processing will cycle between them, the cycle is a specialisation of the cycle of perception and is presented in Figure 10.2. First, the participants in any action being viewed must be isolated. This step will process a newly captured image, using whatever information is available from previously processed images, and will separate the participants from the background and each other. The information so derived will be used to track the movements of the participants, both as they move through the scene and as they move their limbs. We will therefore derive a description of where the people are located and their attitudes. Finally, the interactions performed by the participants must be interpreted. This can only be done with knowledge of the scene being viewed. For example, a system has been developed that interprets American football games, it must know the likely movements of the players in each phase of play so that it is able to recognise their occurrences. The following paragraphs examine these components in more detail.

Isolate Participants

The first operation to be performed on the newly captured data is to separate the regions of the image that correspond to the participants in the activity. There may be more than one participant, in which case we

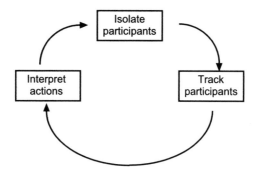

Figure 10.2 The cycle of perception adapted to movement understanding

must also separate the different participants. Occasionally, it is deemed useful to project the location of the participant's image regions into the scene and hence determine their world co-ordinates. The pinhole camera model discussed previously may be used to compute the orientation of the vector from the camera centre to the participant's feet. We must also know the height of the camera above the ground plane (the surface on which the participants are standing, for simplicity, this is often assumed to be planar, but need not be). The intersection of the orientation vector and the ground plane defines the participant's location.

The simplest method of locating a person in an image, is to ensure that an image devoid of people is available. Any difference between the current, "live", image and this "background" image, is therefore due to the participants, Figure 10.3. This simplistic approach is surprisingly effective, provided that the camera never moves with respect to the scene and the background never alters (i.e. the background image never becomes outdated).

The difference between the live, $l(i,j)$, and background, $b(i,j)$, images is computed by:

$$d(i,j) = \begin{cases} 1 & if \ |b(i,j) - l(i,j)| > \theta \\ 0 & otherwise \end{cases}$$

The threshold, θ, is chosen to allow some latitude in the computation of the difference image. The live and background images may differ due to small changes in illumination, comparing the difference against a threshold will prevent these differences being flagged. However, this method produces false positive results for large changes in the scene's illumination and when there is motion of objects that are not participants in the scene.

This algorithm fails completely if there are global changes in the live image. For example, if the background image was captured in daytime and was being compared against a live image captured at night time, every pixel in the image would be different, irrespective of whether the

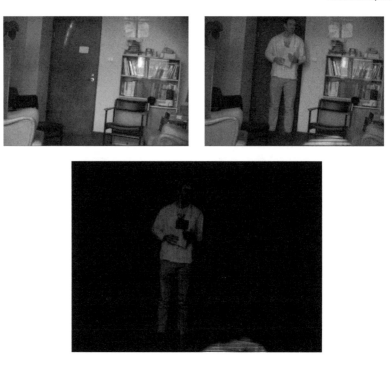

Figure 10.3 Locating participants by image differencing. A static image is compared with a live image. The difference image indicates the presence of a participant in this instance. The pixels that differ could be identified and used as a mask to find the participant in the live image

difference was real or not. A less extreme situation would occur if minor illumination changes occurred, for example, a light being turned on or off, or the sun being obscured by clouds.

The algorithm may be made slightly more robust by updating the background image periodically. The pixels that will contribute to the update will be those that are not significantly different to the background image, i.e. those that have not been identified as belonging to a participant.

$$if\, d(i, j) = \begin{cases} 1 \text{ then } b_{t+1} = b_t \\ 0 \text{ then } b_{t+1} = (1 - \alpha)b_t + \alpha l_{t+1} \end{cases}$$

By changing the value of the parameter α, the speed with which the background image responds to changes in the ambient illumination can be controlled. Making α zero will prevent the background image being updated, making it 1 will cause changes to be propagated without delay. However, this approach still includes an arbitrarily chosen threshold. There is no objective method of choosing a value for this threshold, it must instead be determined by trial and error.

A probabilistic method of assessing the significance of the differences between the pixels of the live and background images has been suggested. This method again depends on capturing background data without participants being present in the scene. The background data is more than a single image, it will consist of the mean and variance/covariance (Σ) of the colour of each pixel. Therefore, the background data will consist of the expected colour and range of colour values for each pixel. When a live image is captured, the likelihood of a difference between the images being due to a real difference, rather than random fluctuations in the data may be computed using the Mahalanobis distance:

$$d(i,j) = (b(i,j)) - l(i,j))^T \Sigma^{-1} (b(i,j) - l(i,j))$$

This distance is the multidimensional equivalent of the standardised statistical distance (which is the difference between a measurement and the average of the measurements, divided by the standard deviation of those measurements). If there is no real difference between the live and background images, there is a 1 in 20 chance of observing a distance of 2 or more, purely due to random variations in the data. The likelihood falls to about a 1 in 100 chance of observing a distance of 3 or more. It is therefore possible to set a threshold to the distance, and suggest that any distance greater than say 2.5 is probably due to a real difference between the live and background images – a participant has entered the scene. The advantage of this approach over the previous method, is that the arbitrary threshold has been replaced by a statistically derived threshold.

It is again possible to gradually update the background image, to compensate for gradual changes in ambient illumination. Those pixels having a distance value less than the threshold are eligible to contribute to the update. The update again adds a proportion of the new pixels' values to the background image. In this way the background image is maintained up to date, without sudden changes.

The thresholded distance image may be used to mask the regions of the live image that correspond to the scene's participants. Separate connected regions (i.e. contiguous groups of pixels) will correspond to the participants. We may further divide each participant's region to identify his or her limbs. A clustering approach may be taken, using the pixels' locations and colours as the variables to be clustered. The resulting clusters may be identified with the head, torso and four limbs of the person in the scene. The clusters may be described using their centroids, measures of elongation (i.e. length of the major and minor axes if the clusters are approximated by ellipses) and their colours.

Track Participants

Now that we are able to locate the participants in an image, we must identify the matching participants in successive images of a sequence. We shall then be able to attempt to understand the activities occurring in the scene we are viewing. Two approaches may be taken to solving the matching problem. In the first, the motion of each cluster in the image sequence is used to predict the cluster's location in the next frame. The cluster nearest to the predicted location is then suggested as the match. In the second approach, the characteristics of the cluster are used to match clusters according to their similarities. The second method is generally better when there are few clusters. If there are n clusters in each image, and assuming that there is a one to one mapping between the clusters then we must perform $O(n^2)$ comparisons to match the clusters. Obviously this number will grow rapidly as the number of clusters increases and will quickly become too large for the comparisons to be made within the available time. Once this has occurred, it will be more efficient to perform predictive matching.

Predictive Tracking

Having located clusters in more than one frame, we may estimate the velocity projected into the image plane of the object (which will be a limb, or a torso, or a head, etc.) that gave rise to the cluster. It is possible to estimate the cluster's acceleration, but this is not usually needed, since we do not need a perfectly accurate prediction of the cluster's location. Given this model of the cluster's movement, the position of the centroid at a time Δt later may be predicted:

$$\hat{p}_{t+\Delta t} = p_t + v_t \Delta t$$

The cluster whose centroid is closest to this predicted position, is the best match. If there is any difference between the predicted and actual locations of the centroid, then the velocity is updated. The cluster characteristics (size and colour, etc) must be used to resolve any conflict in the matching, which would arise if one cluster in one image matches more than one cluster in the other image.

Statistical Matching

Statistical matching uses some of the clusters' characteristics to find the most similar pairs of clusters. Naturally, the clusters' centroids are not useful, as we are attempting to match clusters that may have moved. But the clusters' colours and shape parameters may be used. The values that are computed for the colour and shape parameters may not be very accurate estimates of the true values because the participant will be projected to a small cluster in the image. This uncertainty will not cause the matching to fail, provided that it is smaller than the difference between the participants.

Whichever method we use to identify the matching clusters, the result is a trajectory of that cluster through the image sequence. That is, we have identified the locus of that cluster. The locus may be used to describe the activities that have occurred in the scene.

Participants' Actions and Interactions

The actions and interactions between the actors in a scene can only be understood if the characteristic movements of the activity being viewed have been described. For example, if we were attempting to describe a rugby match, the typical movements of the players in each phase of play would have to be described. A description of the locus of the participants could then be matched against the stored description, the best match would describe that participant's actions.

As a simpler example, we may monitor a public space in a security application. The expected loci of people behaving in particular ways could be described. For example, a person walking purposefully to a destination would have a linear locus. A person loitering would have a more convoluted locus.

Despite this simplistic description, understanding human action is an extremely complex process. Some researchers have succeeded in developing systems that are able to describe the actions of people involved in simple tasks in restricted domains of activity. No-one has yet developed a system that can reliably determine a person's actions, or the interactions of two or more people from a sequence of images.

Information Delivery Systems

Information delivery systems form a very different type of interactive multimedia system. They would typically be used in applications in which information was to be imparted to clients in a public setting. Advertising kiosks would be very attractive if implemented in this way. Other examples are easily invented.

The fact that these information systems are situated in public spaces has consequences for the input data. Most importantly, the clients cannot be expected to behave in any predefined manner. The systems must therefore interpret the behaviours in a flexible way. In practice, this implies that a restricted range of simple behaviours may be recognised. It is likely that a small number of basic behaviours needs to be recognised.

This section of the chapter will discuss the data that may be input to the systems, how the systems will recognise potential clients and attract their attention, and how a "conversation" may be controlled.

Source Data

The characteristics of the source data are governed by the size and shape of the information point since all visual input will be via a camera or cameras mounted on the kiosk. Potential and actual clients will be imaged using the same cameras, and will therefore be viewed at differing resolutions. This has consequences for the types of behaviours that may be recognised, and the structures that we may be able to see. For example, at a large distance, the client's face cannot be resolved. This is not a problem, since at large distances we would want to identify potential clients, face information is not required for this.

To identify potential clients, we may use one of the differencing algorithms already described. We may also determine the client's locations in space using a pair of input cameras. If we know the location of the client in each image and the relative locations and orientations of the cameras, then we may triangulate to determine the client's spatial co-ordinates (Fig. 10.4).

Audio input may also be useful if the kiosk is to support a conversation. However, a single microphone will be of limited use, it would have to be an omnidirectional microphone because we cannot predict the client's location. This type of microphone will then capture all of the sounds in its vicinity, the required voice input as well as the non-required ambient noise. The problem may be overcome by using a phased array of omnidirectional microphones (Fig. 10.5). The outputs of the individual microphones are progressively delayed by equal amounts. Varying the delay will steer the line of maximum sensitivity of the array. If a speaker is identified by processing the visual input, we may steer the array to capture the optimum audio signal.

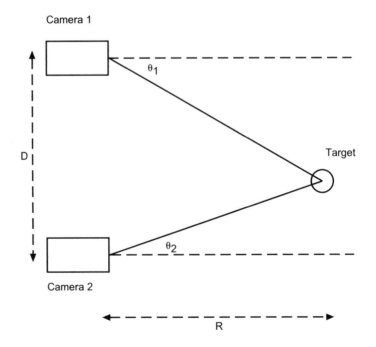

Figure 10.4 Triangulating a potential client to determine his or her range from an information kiosk

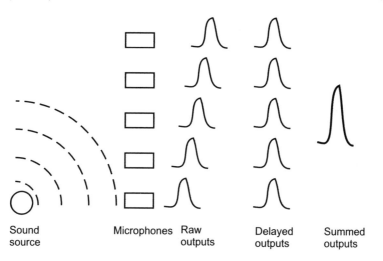

Figure 10.5 A phased array of microphones, illustrating how they may be "steered" to orient their line of maximum sensitivity towards a speaker

Recognising Potential Clients

Potential clients will be recognised in the periphery of the system's active area. This could be at any distance greater than five metres for example, and less than fifteen metres. The region of the image data corresponding to this range will be inspected for potential clients.

A differencing technique may be used to identify the clients. Any region significantly different to the background image may be characterised as a coloured blob. The distribution of colours in the blob must be recorded, as must the apparent size and shape of the blob. This is the minimum information that is required to obtain a correspondence between blobs found in the stereo images. The spatial co-ordinates of the blob may then be found by triangulation. The attention of the potential client may be captured by the system.

Active Participation

To be of use, the system must attract clients to itself. This is usually achieved by having the system call out to the potential clients, to attract their attention and to divert them to the system. Once the client's attention has been captured, the system is able to perform its intended function which could be to advertise some product or to impart useful information.

Feedback

The systems must appear to the clients to be friendly and must provide intelligent feedback, both to indicate that the client's requests have been understood and to indicate which client is the focus of attention – if several are present.

Most systems of this type will use an avatar to provide feedback. This is a synthetic head and face. The face can be animated in synchrony with any audio output. The avatar can be used to indicate which client is the focus of attention, by having it turn its head and fixate on that client. The avatar can also be given human-like behaviours to increase its acceptability. The use of avatars will be discussed further in the following chapter.

Video Surveillance and Monitoring

Two types of system have been discussed in this chapter, one that simply tracked the participants in a scene and attempted to infer their actions, the other initiated a dialogue with any participant who entered the system's field of view. In this section, we shall discuss the potential uses of movement interpretation systems. The areas of potential use have been divided into those applications in which the scene's geometry is known, and those applications in which it is unknown.

Monitoring Known Scenes

A known scene is one in which the camera's location and orientation are known, as are the relevant aspects of the geometry of the scene being viewed by the camera. As shown in Figure 10.6, the system must be calibrated with the height of the camera's optical centre above the ground plane and the camera's orientation with respect to the ground plane. For accurate work, the topography of the surface must also be known, but most applications can assume that the surface is a horizontal plane. Given this information, what knowledge can be derived about people and objects moving about in the scene?

Monitoring systems are likely to be used in situations where the instantaneous locations of moving objects are required. These locations will be interpreted using information about the static structures in the scene. As an example, we shall consider a system that is intended to monitor a corridor and provide a commentary about the activities occurring in the corridor: the system could suggest when someone was lingering outside a doorway, or a person was passing along the corridor. The "static structures" would be the doorways in the corridor, the entrances and exits. Although the example considers people's activities in a corridor, the techniques that we discuss are equally applicable to the analysis of any known scene.

To generate the commentary, we must know the locations of people within the corridor. The first task of the system is to identify the pixels in the image that correspond to people. This can be done using one of the simple differencing techniques discussed above. Then we must estimate

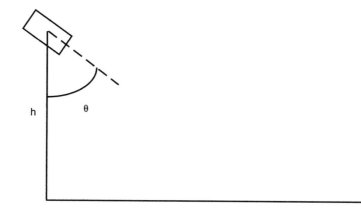

Figure 10.6 The scene geometry for monitoring known scenes

the person's location in the corridor. Two ways of deriving this information have been suggested: either by inspecting the image data, or by transforming the image data into a plan view.

The person's location may be derived directly from the image data by identifying the lowest pixel(s) of the person region. Assuming that this pixel corresponds to a part of the person that is in contact with the ground, we may use the pinhole camera model to compute a direction vector from the camera to that pixel. The intersection of this vector with the ground plane defines the person's location. Naturally, the estimate of location is uncertain and the largest source of uncertainty will be the location of the lowest pixel: does it really correspond to the point of contact of the person and the ground? Errors in this location will place the person closer to or further away from the camera. The magnitude of the uncertainty can be reduced by increasing the resolution of the imaging system.

Transforming the image data to a plan view may present the information in a more understandable fashion. In this example, the boundaries of the walls and floor of the corridor will be transformed into a pair of parallel lines, the locations of people moving about in the corridor will be transformed into points in the plan view. The transformation is performed by rotating the image data; effectively rotating the camera location to a point vertically above the scene. The location of people in the corridor is again determined by finding the point of contact of the person and the floor. The point is then moved to its location in the rotated image.

A comment may be added to the commentary about the person's location and movements, once the person's location in the scene has been computed. If the person has not moved for a certain number of frames of data, then perhaps they are looking for a room along the corridor, if the person has moved a consistent amount between frames, we may infer that they are moving purposefully along the corridor.

Two further issues must be discussed. How should the "static struc-tures" of the corridor be determined? And how should we determine the loci of people in the corridor when it is crowded?

A meaningful commentary can only be generated given a knowledge of the static structures in the scene: the boundaries of the floor and the locations of entry and exit points, i.e. doorways. These may be indicated manually or automatically in a preliminary set-up procedure. Manual set-up would be achieved simply by annotating the camera's image, once the camera had been correctly positioned. Automatically annotating the image is a more interesting problem that will involve identifying the static struc-tures by their image properties. The process would involve identifying the walls and floor of the corridor using their colour and texture properties, and then locating the doors in the walls, recognising that the doors will be projected rectangles, probably of a different colour to the walls.

The second problem to be addressed is that of generating the loci of people as they move along the corridor. The problem can be reformu-lated as identifying the matching people in a sequence of images that may contain one or more people who may or may not match. That is, we may observe people entering and leaving the corridor and moving along it. This is a trivial problem if only one person is present, but becomes more difficult when the regions of the image that correspond to the people in the corridor begin to overlap. In that case we must separate the multiple person region into the individuals. Provided that the indi-viduals are sufficiently different and that none is totally obscured, this can be achieved by inspecting a single image. If the region cannot be resolved into the constituent people, we would have to infer the position of the obscured people by inspecting their locations in the preceding and succeeding images. Provided that the persons' movements are smooth, we may interpolate their locations in the images in which they are obscured, Figure 10.7.

Finally, how is the system calibrated? The obvious method would be by measurement, we have to measure the height of the camera above the ground and measure its orientation. But calibration could also be performed automatically by placing objects in known relative positions. By inverting the location computations, the position information can be used to determine the characteristics of the system.

Monitoring Unknown Scenes

An unknown scene differs from a known scene in that the camera's location with respect to objects in the scene is not known. That is, we do not know the camera's orientation nor height above the ground. The consequence of this is that we cannot estimate the absolute spatial co-ordinates of any object in the image. However, a meaningful commentary can still be generated, but without using distance measurements (it could

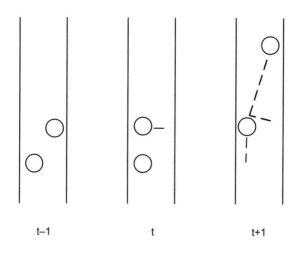

Figure 10.7 Resolution of multiple person regions by inspecting the locus of the people. The missing locations are interpolated from the previous and next known positions. This diagram shows a plan view, in a view taken along the corridor there will be instances in which one person obscures the other

be argued that this is a more natural commentary, since we do not often use distance measures when describing a scene, instead we use phrases like "close to", "nearby" or "adjacent to", etc).

The systems can be used equally well for scene monitoring, but we cannot compute a plan view of the scene being inspected. We can however regain some information about the scene. First we must annotate the image, a process that labels regions of the image as, for example, wall or floor. Thereafter we may isolate people in the scene and describe their actions with respect to the labelled objects.

The major difficulty in this activity is the initial labelling of the scene. The goals of labelling are to define regions of the image that correspond to surfaces on which we can stand and to identify landmarks that will be useful for the commentary. Again, labelling may be performed manually or automatically using the same methods as previously described.

Finally, we could argue that no scene need be unknown. The final paragraph of the preceding section suggested that the camera position and orientation could be computed if objects were placed in known locations. Figure 10.8 summarises the measurements, three objects are placed with known separations. Their orientations in the image are measured. This information can be used to determine the camera's positional parameters. Naturally, this approach is only valid when the objects are placed in the same horizontal plane, and will be limited to determining the projection of unknown objects onto that plane.

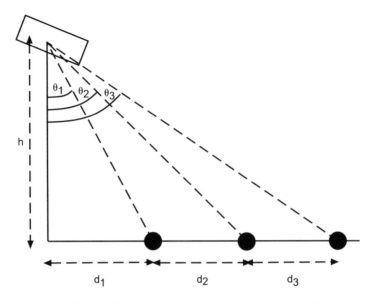

Figure 10.8 Camera calibration. The height of the camera above the ground, and its orientation can be determined if objects are place in known positions

Conclusion

This chapter has described multimedia systems whose deployment is not restricted to the laboratory, the home or workplace. Rather, the systems are to be deployed where potential users are completely free to interact with them at will. Two types of systems have been described, one passively observes a scene interpreting the actions occurring in it. The other type of system actively seeks the participation of clients in some form of dialogue. Neither type of system has yet been developed to a working version, the chapter has described some of the approaches being taken to developing the systems and has highlighted some of the problems associated with these types of system. The final section of the chapter examined surveillance and monitoring systems.

Bibliography

Printed Material

Waters K, Rehg R, Loughlin M, Kang SB, Terzopoulos D (1998) "Visual sensing of humans for active public interfaces", in *Computer Vision for Human-Machine Interaction*, Cipolla R, Pentland A (eds), CUP, Cambridge.

Wren C, Azarbayejani A, Darrell T, Pentland A (1997) "pFinder: Real-Time Tracking of the Human Body", *IEEE Trans Pattern Analysis and Machine Intelligence*, vol. 19:780–85.

Internet Resources

MIT Media laboratory   http://www.media.mit.edu/

11 Synthesising a Visual Response

Introduction

In this final chapter, the issue of generating visual output will be examined. The output will consist of the system's responses to the user. Naturally, the outputs will vary in complexity according to the tasks being performed by the system, but will fall in to one of two types. One type of output will simply be to echo the user's input, this output is given as feedback to reassure the user that the system has understood the input. The other type of output will consist of the system's responses to the user's inputs, that is, the system's half of a dialogue. This second category of response implies that the system has comprehended the input, processed it and formulated an appropriate response. The mechanisms of generating the response are outside of the scope of this discussion, what is relevant are the methods of delivering the response. The chapter will discuss very briefly the uses and types of feedback a system should provide. The use of synthetic faces to "speak" to the user will be introduced and justified. This is followed by an overview of the range of methods used to generate and animate heads, and a more extensive discussion of two current systems that capture head data and animate it.

Feedback

Any computer system must provide feedback to its users. The feedback should be at several levels. At the highest level, a system should provide an indication that it has completed its intended task, successfully or not, and should deliver its results. Crudely, a system should provide an output, otherwise it serves no purpose. At the lowest level, a system should respond to the immediate inputs in two ways:

1. the system should give an indication that it has received the input. This is equivalent to the click sound that is played when a button is pressed, or the button's colour being changed momentarily.
2. the system should demonstrate its interpretation of the instruction – the equivalent of a respondent repeating or paraphrasing your instructions. This is especially important if the system has to process input to derive the instructions.

The purpose of this low level feedback is to provide the user with information that will either reassure him that the input was correctly interpreted, or to help him to modify the input and so to correct the system's erroneous interpretation. The methods of providing the feedback will be dependent on the system itself. The simplest feedback is provided by head pointing devices. This type of system must simply move the onscreen cursor to its estimate of the location indicated by the user. The cursor location itself is the only feedback that the system needs to provide. It enables the user to rapidly correct for any system errors, and also for the user to compensate for systematic errors. This example is trivial and not in the scope of this chapter.

A more complex method of providing feedback is to use a computer-generated head that will "speak" the computer generated textual response. Imagine navigating through a multimedia presentation. Each page presents some alternative further destinations. The choice is usually presented in a visual format, either as a textual description of each of the destinations, or as an iconic representation. This model assumes that the presentation is delivered using a traditional platform, and the response will be obtained by the user moving the cursor and clicking on the required button (compare the problem of navigating WWW hyperlinks).

Now imagine a non-traditional delivery platform without the usual mouse to control the cursor. The presentation of choices will change because the user will indicate the choices differently. How can the navigational options be presented? And, how are the user's choices to be indicated? The question is applicable to any multimedia system that is being delivered using atypical hardware (i.e. no mouse).

A simple answer would be to model a conversational interface (the implementation of this answer may not be simple!). The client speaks to the application, the application speaks to the client. The application will have to be able to understand the client's speech, at least at a rudimentary level, perhaps looking for key words or phrases. It will also have to present material in a friendly manner. Having a simulated head to speak a description of the choices and presenting an abbreviated summary textually will achieve this goal.

The second example concerns the problem of video conferencing. A typical videoconference has participants at diverse locations. Video (sound and image) data is captured at each location and transmitted to all of the others. This requires substantial communication bandwidth between the venues which is not readily available, witness the fact that high quality videoconferencing facilities are sparsely distributed. As a means of reducing the bandwidth, and thereby increasing the number of potential videoconference facilities, consider the case where images of each attendant are captured and transmitted once only to the receiver where they are used to build graphical models of the attendees. During the course of the conference, parameters are derived from the attendees' images, and used to animate the models.

The shared characteristics of these examples are the synthesis and animation of a head model. These two activities are the subjects of the remainder of the chapter. The aim of these processes is to generate an animated head that appears to be realistic. The degree of realism is a matter of debate, practitioners will always aim for the highest degree of realism. Conversely, the users of these systems, seeing that the best animated heads are far from being realistic seem to want subrealistic systems, that is, systems that are purposefully given a slightly synthetic appearance.

An Overview of Methods of Generating and Animating Head Models

We may identify three basic requirements for facial animations. These concern the movements of the mouth, the other facial features and the face itself.

The animation must move the mouth in synchrony with the speech signal. That is, the mouth must open and close in time with the words. The shape of the mouth must change in accordance with the sounds being produced. This is not so obvious as relating a mouth shape to each phoneme. When we considered speech generation and recognition we encountered the coarticulation problem – speech sounds are influenced by the preceding and succeeding sounds. This is equally true for facial animation systems, when making some sounds, the mouth has already assumed the shape required for the following sound. Therefore, the speech signal must be processed using a look-ahead technique to discover these instances. Consider the shape the mouth takes when making the "l" sound, it is dependent on the following phoneme (think of "look" and "like").

If the facial animation was restricted to pasting a moving mouth onto a static face, we would be left with an extremely unnatural effect. In normal conversation, a person's whole face is involved. The eyes and eyebrows are especially used for emphasising the spoken words. So the rest of the face must be sympathetically animated. The eyebrows should be moved up or down to emphasise what is being said, the extent of the movement should be in proportion to the sense of what is being said, otherwise the model will overact. The eyes should be rotated and should occasionally blink or close, some of these movements will be deliberate, others will appear random, to simulate saccadic movements or involuntary blinks. The rate of blinking can also provide a clue as to the emotional involvement of the speaker with his words. It is tempting from a computational viewpoint to consider the mouth, eyes and eyebrows as separate entities whose movements have no influence on each other. However, the face is covered in an elastic skin that wrinkles and stretches as a consequence of facial movements. The third requirement is that other parts of the face should bulge or wrinkle as the mouth changes shape or the eyebrows are moved. The accumulation of these synchronised movements will give expression and life to the animation.

Generating Head Models

No synthetic head can be animated without an underlying model. The model must include information regarding the shape of the head, its colours and textures and how its component parts may move. Figure 11.1 summarises the major steps of the process of generating a static head model.

Head Shape

The head must be given a basic shape that resembles a generic head. This shape may be fixed or may be perturbed to resemble a specific person. A fixed head shape is appropriate for a system that is to model a single head, a personal assistant for example. A flexible system is needed in

Head image with superimposed
triangulation points

Figure 11.1 Triangulation of a head image. In practice a number of head images would be captured from different locations. The same points must be indicated in each of the images, several hundred may be required. The points will then be linked into a network of triangles. The triangles will model the head surface

videoconferencing applications, for example, where instances of multiple users are required.

The generic head shape need be derived once only. Heads may be measured either by scanning volunteers' heads or by using computer vision techniques to recover three-dimensional information from a number of images of heads taken from a multitude of orientations. Using either approach, the spatial co-ordinates of many points on the head surface are determined. These points are triangulated, that is, they are linked into a network of triangles or sometimes polygons. The triangles are the basic data structure used to render the head image.

One sample head is sufficient to create a usable model, but it will not be universally applicable, as there is a wide range of head appearances. Many samples of heads should be captured, to create models typical of each generic head type. Having many samples of each head type enables us to estimate not only the mean head but also the modes of variation in head shape. This is useful in systems requiring the head model to match the user, a closely matching model may be computed.

Figure 11.1 suggests how the process of generating a head model from a set of images is performed. The figure shows one image pair, in practice several are needed. The locations of the same set of points are indicated in each of the images. The larger the number of points, the better the final rendered image, and the more computation is required to generate it. As a compromise, the concentration of points is higher around the important facial features – the eyes, nose and mouth. Given several images and, the way the camera was moved in between taking the images, the spatial co-ordinates of the points in the images may be computed. The points may then be triangulated. The polygon or triangle mesh forms the basic data structure for representing the head. The diagram has suggested a small number of triangles, in practice, hundreds would be used. Triangulating by hand is a laborious process.

Head Appearance

We may render a model of the shape of the head using any of the standard graphical techniques. This will involve assigning colour and reflectivity properties to each of the triangles of the model and specifying the lighting conditions. A shaded model is then generated, which lacks realism as it does not contain any of the textural properties of the human skin: no skin blemishes, no facial hair, etc. An improved model is generated by mapping images of a real person onto the head shape. The degree of realism so generated is dependent on the number of images that are texture mapped, since the resulting animation lacks reality at the borders of the mapped texture images.

Head Movement

The movement of the component parts of the head can be modelled either by capturing the motion of real heads or by modelling the mechanisms by which real heads are moved, i.e. how muscle groups contract to move face parts, what effect does this have on the overlying skin. This topic is the subject of the following section.

Animating Head Models

How the animation is performed depends on the underlying animation model. We have either to determine how the skin surface should move and deform in response to the movements required to make mouth shapes that match the speech. Or we must move the underlying musculature and have the surface more in consequence. There are at least five fundamental approaches to facial animation: key framing, performance driven, direct parameterisation, pseudo-muscle based and muscle based animations. All of the methods aim to manipulate the surface of the face over time such that the faces have the desired expressions that resemble real expressions.

Key Framing Animation

Key framing is a technique in which a database of mouth shapes is created. The database could also include other facial features. The images will be the shape of the mouth when articulating the phonemes or diphones used in the speech model. The animation will be performed by selecting the appropriate sequence of images based on the sequence of phonemes generated by the speech generating process. Intervening images will be interpolated.

Direct Parameterisation Animation

These techniques incorporate a model of the head's possible movements. The various movements are driven by user defined parameters. To animate the head model, the user must define the temporal development of the parameters' values. Whilst this is a very laborious method to follow, it can yield very high quality results, provided that the user understands the interactions of the parameters, and the effects that they achieve.

Performance Driven Animation

The major disadvantage of parameterised animation techniques is the large number of parameters to be manipulated. It is hugely important that the parameters change at the correct rates and times, otherwise they will combine to give unrealistic expressions. Performance driven animation systems simplify this complexity by adding an interface layer that hides the parameter values from the user. The user is presented with an interface that specifies the type and extent of the emotions to be displayed. Whilst this may lead to each emotion being displayed in exactly the same manner, it does ease the problem of creating the animations. The parameters are usually divided into two sets, those that control the topology of the face and those that control its expression.

Animating faces using this approach is much simpler than controlling the entire set of parameters; parameterisation animation has therefore been absorbed into this method.

Muscle and Pseudo Muscle Based Animation

The facial anatomy is extremely complex, too complex to be modelled directly. These techniques simplify the anatomy and represent the face as a two dimensional network of springs. The lengths and elasticities of the springs determine the shape of the static face, and its dynamic properties, i.e. how one part of the face deforms in response to a change in muscle tension elsewhere. The total muscle force on a point is made up of contributions due to:

1. the neighbouring points in the spring network;
2. the restoring force due to the point's displacement;
3. any external forces due to muscles acting on the point;
4. any viscosity preventing the point returning instantaneously to its rest location.

By setting the external forces appropriate to a particular expression or mouth shape, a surface of the complete face may be computed.

Tracking a Human Actor

Whilst the prospect of generating an animated synthetic head from a model is attractive, there are applications in which the modelled head is to mimic the head movements of a human. The example already cited of the videoconference is one of these situations. In this application, the attendees are viewed by a system that attempts to infer their expression as well as the dynamic properties of their faces. This information is transmitted to the other participants in the conference where it is synthesised into the modelled face.

This technique is not strictly an animation technique, but is included here as it can be used in some applications.

Incorporating Expression

It is useful to be able to separate the animation of the mouth and the rest of the face. The mouth moves in response to the words being spoken. The rest of the face emphasises the meaning and emotion contained in the words. The two movements can be considered independently.

Facial Animation Systems

This last section of the chapter will describe two functioning facial animation systems that incorporate all of the previously discussed elements.

System One

This system is provided with a generic three-dimensional head model. A realistic and personal head model is made by capturing one front and one profile photograph of an intended user. Computer vision techniques are used to locate in three dimensions the positions of salient features that describe the shape of the face. This information is used to conform a generic head model. The two images are then texture mapped onto the head model. The system thus creates a texture-mapped model of the user. The model has the same shape and visual appearance.

Animation of the head model is driven by the annotated phoneme sequence derived from the text to speech system. (The annotated phoneme sequence is used in that system as an intermediate representation, the text is transformed into a stream of phonemes annotated with emphases, which is further transformed into the signals to be used by the speech synthesiser). The sequence is to be used to derive a sequence of mouth and face movements. Initially, the movement sequence is built by selecting motion primitives from a database of facial motions which are joined to form a sequence of frames – a movie sequence.

More attention is paid to the perceptually important face regions, in this case these are the mouth movements and facial expressions. Muscle models have been used to create simple expressions such as smiling, surprise, anger and delight.

System Two

The possible face movements have been categorised according to their functionality. One set of movements is due to the speech itself, these are movements of the mouth and are controlled by the stream of phonemes. A second set of movements is due to the speaker's intonation. These movements clarify and expand on the words being spoken and include:

1. conversational signals, an accumulation of rapid movements such as more pronounced mouth movements, blinks or head movements which are used to clarify and support the speech;
2. punctuators, movements associated with punctuation in the text: pauses and slower movements;
3. regulators, that aid the interactions between speaker and listener: co-ordinated head and eye movements;
4. manipulators, movements that correspond to the biological needs of the face, such as blinking to moisten the eyes.

The categories are functionally independent, but may involve the same features, eyebrow movements are involved in most movements. The movements of the various face components are determined as the accumulation of the movements due to each category.

The system takes as input the familiar annotated stream of phonemes. The phonemes define the sequence of mouth shapes that must be followed. Each phoneme would define a particular mouth shape in the absence of coarticulation. Given that one phoneme influences the effects of its predecessor, the system inspects the current and next phonemes before assigning a mouth shape.

The annotations are used to infer the effects due to the functional categories. The emotion symbols define the onset, intensity and duration of each emotion that must be signified. The effects of the conversational signals are then computed, then the punctuators' effects in the conversational pauses are added in – these facial expressions will vary according to the basic emotion. Manipulator actions must occur independently of all others since they are involuntary actions not under the speaker's conscious control.

Conclusions

This chapter has been concerned with methods of providing visual feedback to users of multimedia systems. In particular we have examined methods of generating animated head models, that is animations of a head that are able to display expressions and to make the correct facial movements for an accompanying speech signal. The most advanced systems are beginning to be deployed in practical situations. Current systems lack realism. They have lower resolution than is necessary to generate realistic images. The image properties lack realism, that is, lighting effects appear unnatural, as do the movements of the models. The authors of head animations are continually striving for increased realism. However, the consumers are aware that they are viewing a model and do not appear to require it to be too realistic: the model must have a slightly synthetic appearance. It is important that the users of these systems are aware that it is a computer-generated head that is speaking.

Animated faces have numerous applications. It was suggested earlier that they could be used in videoconferencing, each participant in the videoconference would be represented by a model in a virtual conference room, and the models could be generated from the participants. Each participant would see the virtual conference room from their model's viewpoint. Animated heads could also be used as the outward expression of an intelligent assistant, they would deliver the information generated by the assistant, which could be a commentary of the activities occurring in a scene (Chapter 10), or something as mundane as reading emails.

Animated heads continue to be improved. First, systems are becoming more realistic, even if there is little call for this at the moment. Second, systems are being extended to animating more than the head. Ultimately, whole body animations will be produced.

Bibliography

Printed Material

Angel E (1997) Interactive Computer Graphics, Addison–Wesley, Reading MA.
Parke FI, Waters K (1996) Computer Facial Animation, AK Peters, Natick, MA.
Watt A, Policarpo F (1998) The Computer Image, Addison-Wesley, Harlow.

Internet Resources

British Telecom has developed several applications using these ideas, reports are accessible via: http://www.labs.bt.com/projects/
Other resources are linked from the UCSC Perceptual Science Laboratory: http://mambo.ucsc.edu/psl/fan.html

12 Conclusions

This book has been concerned with multimedia systems, that is, those computer systems in which interaction with a user occurs via channels other than the keyboard and screen. We have examined the requirements for capturing, storing and replaying perceptually realistic information. We have discussed methods of designing and delivering multimedia content to consumers. But the largest section of the book has been concerned with an examination of the methods of realising interactive multimedia systems. These systems are currently limited in use and deployment – and two reasons may be responsible for this. First, the methods by which multimedia data should be processed to extract the required information are not yet clearly defined. Second, current widely available hardware is not capable of processing the data sufficiently fast to allow multimedia interaction to be used to support other applications, such as word processing or graphical editors.

The Current State of Multimedia Systems

At present, multimedia delivery systems are widely available, and widely used, in education, entertainment and industry. The presentations they deliver can appear to be very sophisticated, containing many visual and aural effects. However, the underlying structure of the presentation is much simpler than its appearance would suggest. The information to be presented has been organised into related items that are presented on single pages. The designer has also organised the links between pages that allow the viewer to navigate his or her path through the presentation. Progression between pages will be achieved by the user clicking on-screen buttons or by using the computer keyboard.

The data objects to be shown by a multimedia presentation will have been carefully chosen to enhance the presentation and will have been manipulated to appear as realistic as possible, given the presentation hardware. However, the objects being presented will lack realism, simply because our ability to perceive sound and images far exceeds the capacity of most computer systems to deliver them.

The single dominant characteristic of these presentation systems is that they are computer centred. They use the computer as a delivery platform: the user communicates (in a rudimentary fashion) with the system using the mouse and keyboard for input and the screen and sound system for output. Engineers at Microsoft have termed this type of interaction "worshipping at the altar", the phrase describes the physical attitude of the user and the mental attitude – the computer system is dominant.

A few multimedia systems have been developed that challenge this attitude, by allowing the user to communicate with the computer via alternative channels. These systems are still experimental, but allow the user to control computer systems by voice commands or by gestures. In addition, the computer systems are able to communicate with the user using other, more human centred communication channels, such as voice output.

Whilst human centred computing is seen as a desirable target, there are two major obstacles inhibiting its achievement. First, processor capacity limits the volume of data that may be manipulated. Second, the methods by which multimedia data may be processed to reliably achieve the required functionality have yet to be discovered.

A multimedia system must interpret multimedia input data in addition to performing the task required of it, much like any current operating system must interpret mouse movements and clicks. This will require the system to process large amounts of data, for example using video input could require a data throughput of some tens of megabytes per second if every pixel is to be manipulated in real-time. This throughput is in addition to the processing required for the task being performed, e.g. word processing a document. This throughput rate can be reduced by sensible design of the software, but it will remain very high, high enough to restrict the range of applications that may be used. However, the power of computer processors has increased exponentially over the last twenty years, and this increase is expected to continue. Therefore, the limitations imposed by processor power on current systems will eventually be overcome.

Previous chapters have demonstrated how sound signals may be interpreted as speech, and how video signals may be processed to decode gestures or movements. The data that is manipulated must be captured under carefully controlled conditions. For example, it is not yet possible to isolate and interpret one speaker's words from a sound signal containing many speakers' voices, nor is it yet possible to reliably isolate a person's hands and fingers when seen against a confusing background. When processing such data one must ensure that only one speaker's voice is captured, or the background contrasts with the objects being sought.

Multimedia interpretation systems also have difficulties with following the data reliably, for example a gesture interpreting system may lose track of the gestures being made. Systems must be designed to be robust against poor quality or missing data; they must be able to recover from such errors and not only continue to process the data as if there was no loss, but also interpolate the missing data. Undoubtedly these problems will be solved in the near future and we shall be released from communicating with our computers exclusively through the keyboard.

What of the Future?

The future of multimedia systems can be viewed in the short term as a progression of current technological advances. For example, there has been a trend for processors to become smaller and more powerful, this is a trend that is likely to continue for some time and to have consequences on the size and capabilities of multimedia computers.

Not only have processors become more powerful, the peripheral devices of a computer system have also improved. For example, graphical subsystems continue to become capable of rendering ever more realistic images, by virtue of increasing the number of pixels in the images, the colour resolution and the rate at which these images may be drawn. Therefore, the appearance of still and moving images becomes more realistic.

Today, very few computers are operated in isolation, most are interconnected using some form of network. This allows data to be shared between geographically separated users working on the same project, or the same users to communicate by text, speech or images transmitted across the network. As the bandwidth (i.e. the volume of data able to be transmitted per unit of time) of the network has increased, so too has the complexity of the data that may be transmitted. Where once communication was limited to transmitting textual messages, we are now able to broadcast low resolution video data. As the bandwidth of the communication networks increases, the quality of the broadcast data will increase, and its use will increase as users find the quality becomes acceptable (i.e. comparable to the quality that is expected of broadcast material).

A characteristic of today's multimedia systems is that the data is captured by intrusive transducers. Voice data is captured using microphones that must be placed in close proximity to the user's mouth. If image data is used, then the user must be aware of the camera's location and must perform for the camera. Systems will be developed that are aware of the users' locations and can therefore control the data capture process: we may use a phased array of microphones to direct the orientation of the input, or we may devise systems that have multiple camera inputs and can select the most appropriate data for the task being performed and the user's location. This will be the single most significant change in our view of computer systems – it will release us from being tied to a monitor screen and keyboard.

In parallel to the changing input devices, there must be advances in the sophistication of the underlying software. The software has to be aware of the type of data being processed, the range of expected inputs and the ability to deal with input data of differing qualities. In short, the software must have human-like ability to understand the input data. Only then will multimedia systems demonstrate the intelligence required to behave in an unobtrusive fashion.

In conclusion, we may view the future development of multimedia systems as moving away from computer centred systems and towards human centred systems. Multimedia systems must never be seen as an end in themselves, but as an enabling technology. They make other computer systems easier to use because the computer system adapts to the user, rather than forcing the user to adapt to the system.

Appendix 1
HTML – Hypertext Markup Language

Introduction

To describe HTML as a language is misleading, as it is not a language in the sense of other programming languages. HTML consists of a set of *tags* that are embedded within a document to specify how the document should be displayed by a web browser. This has similarities to modern wordprocessor documents that consist of the text to be read plus the formatting information. However, the writing process is fundamentally different, the wordprocessor does not allow you to access the formatting instructions, indeed they are actively hidden from the author; conversely, HTML has been designed to allow authors full control over what tags are used and where. This can be overwhelming, and so HTML editors have been designed that allow the author to design his document graphically, the editor will insert the correct tags at the correct locations to achieve the desired effect.

This Appendix presents enough of the syntax of the Hypertext Markup Language to enable you to design your own webpages without needing to use an HTML editor. This does not set out to be a complete "how to do . . . using HTML" guidebook, other texts are available for this purpose. Instead, this should give you sufficient knowledge of HTML to start to write your own web pages.

A Simple Guide to HTML

HTML is a continually evolving "standard". With each new edition of the standard, new tags are introduced and the use of some old ones discouraged. Consequently, any attempt at describing the nature of HTML will rapidly become incorrect. There is also be a delay between the publication of a new HTML feature and it being supported by web browsers.

Whilst most of HTML is described in this appendix, some of these features may not yet be supported by a particular browser, or may already be outdated!

The following sections describe the overall structure of an HTML document, the mechanisms of controlling the appearance of a document by structuring it and altering fonts, how other documents are linked to the current one, and how lists, forms and frames are created. A final section describes the linking of Java applets into a page.

The Minimal HTML Document

An HTML document should be declared to be one and it must have a head and a body. Within the head it should also be given a title, which will appear as the title of the browser's window when the document is displayed. The minimal HTML document will consist of the following tags:

```
<HTML>
<HEAD>
<TITLE>My document's title
</TITLE>
</HEAD>
<BODY>
</BODY>
</HTML>
```

The document's general appearance will be declared between the two head tags. The author can specify the document's background colour or a background bitmap, the normal colour of text, and the colours of visited, active and not visited links. The bulk of the document's information will be declared between the two body tags.

In this and the following examples, the tags have been written in upper case, most tags are not case sensitive. It is good practice to be consistent in writing tags in one case or the other, this will contribute to making your documents easier to understand and therefore easier to maintain.

Notation

In the remainder of this description of HTML, a simple notation has been used:

URL	the universal resource locator of a file – the file's web address or its name if it is in the same directory as your HTML file.
?	a number, e.g. H? could be H1, H2, H3, etc.
%	a percentage, e.g. WIDTH="%" could mean WIDTH="75" etc.
***	arbitrary text.

$$$$$$	an arbitrary hexadecimal number, usually to specify a colour, in which the digits are taken in pairs and represent the intensities of red, green and blue that make up this colour.
, , ,	comma delimited list, e.g. COORDS=" , , , " implies that four coords need to be supplied.
|	separates alternatives, one of which must be chosen.

Now on to the HTML tags. . . .

Text Formatting

Various text-formatting effects are started and cancelled by enclosing the text to be formatted by the following pairs of tags. It is good practice not to overlap the tags, i.e. to start two effects and cancel them in the same order, instead you should cancel them in the reverse order.

`<B>  </B>`	Bold text
`<I>  </I>`	Italic text
`<U>  </U>`	Underlined text
`<STRIKE>  </STRIKE>`	Crossed out text
`<S>  </S>`	Superscript
`<SUB>  </SUB>`	Subscript
`<TT>  </TT>`	Typewriter – a monospaced effect
`<PRE>  </PRE>`	Preformatted text – displays text as it is written in the HTML source,
`<PRE WIDTH=?>  </PRE>`	the width of the formatting may be altered using the width attribute
`<CENTER>  </CENTER>`	Centre alignment
`<BLINK>  </BLINK>`	Blinking text
`<FONT SIZE =?>  </FONT >`	Alters text size
`<FONT SIZE =+|-?>  </FONT >`	Incrementally alters text size
`<BASEFONT SIZE=?>`	Declares base font size
`<FONT COLOR="#$$$$$$">  </FONT>`	Declares font colour
`<FONT FACE="***"></FONT>`	Declares base font
`<MULTICOL COLS=?>  </MULTICOL>`	Declares multi-column output
`<MULTICOL GUTTER=?>  </MULTICOL>`	Specifies a gutter (margin) width
`<MULTICOL WIDTH=?>  </MULTICOL>`	Specifies a gutter height
`<SPACER>`	The basic spacer tag
`<SPACER TYPE=horizontal |vertical|block>`	Type attribute of spacer

`<SPACER SIZE=?>`	Size attribute of spacer
`<SPACER WIDTH=?` `  HEIGHT=?>`	Dimension attribute of spacer
`<SPACER ALIGN=left|` `  right|center>`	Alignment attribute of spacer

Font Control

These tags are used to control the appearance of text in a document. The exact appearance is governed by the browser's preferences.

`<H?>  </H?>`	Heading (levels 1 to 6)

`<H?`
`ALIGN=LEFT|CENTER|RIGHT>`
`</H?>`
	Heading alignment attribute

`<DIV></DIV>`	Division (subdivides your document)

`<DIV ALIGN=`
`LEFT|RIGHT|CENTER|`
`JUSTIFY></DIV>`
	Division alignment attribute

`<BLOCKQUOTE>` `</BLOCKQUOTE>`	Blockquote
`<EM></EM>`	Emphasis (italicised)
`<STRONG></STRONG>`	Strong emphasis (bold)
`<CITE></CITE>`	Citation
`<CODE></CODE>`	Code (for source code listings)
`<SAMP></SAMP>`	Sample Output
`<KBD></KBD>`	Keyboard Input
`<VAR></VAR>`	Variable
`<DFN></DFN>`	Definition
`<ADDRESS></ADDRESS>`	Author's address
`<BIG></BIG>`	Large font size
`<SMALL></SMALL>`	Small font size

Links and Graphics

Your web page will be linked from one or more other pages, and will also require links to other pages, either as destination pages to visit or the sources of images for your page. This section describes how this is achieved.

`<A HREF="URL"></A>`	a link to a target
`<A HREF="URL#***"></A>`	a link to a target in another document
`<A HREF="#***"></A>`	a link to a target in the current document

`<A HREF="URL"` `TARGET="***"></A>`	a target window (used when a page is displayed using frames)
`<A NAME="***"></A>`	declare a target
`<IMG SRC="URL">`	display an image

`<IMG SRC="URL"`
`ALIGN=TOP|BOTTOM|MIDDLE|`
`LEFT|RIGHT>`
	image alignment attributes

`<IMG SRC="URL"`
`ALIGN=TEXTTOP|ABSMIDDLE|`
`BASELINE|ABSBOTTOM>`
	image alignment attributes

`<IMG SRC="URL"` `ALT="***">`	alternative text (if image is not displayed)
`<IMG SRC="URL" WIDTH=?` `HEIGHT=?>`	image dimensions
`<IMG SRC="URL" BORDER=?>`	image border

`<META HTTP-`
`EQUIV="Refresh"`
`CONTENT="?; URL=URL">`
	Client Pull

`<EMBED SRC="URL">`	embed an object
`<EMBED SRC="URL" WIDTH=?` `HEIGHT=?>`	declare object size

Dividers

This set of tags describes how the paragraphs of a document are declared and separated. If the paragraph tag is omitted, then most browsers will run your paragraphs together.

`<P> </P>`	paragraph tags, the closing tag is often unnecessary
`<P ALIGN=LEFT|CENTER|` `RIGHT> </P>`	paragraph alignment
` `	line break
`<BR CLEAR=LEFT|RIGHT|` `ALL>`	text wrapping
`<HR>`	horizontal line
`<HR ALIGN=LEFT|RIGHT|` `CENTER>`	line's alignment
`<HR SIZE=?>`	line's thickness in pixels
`<HR WIDTH=?>`	line's width in pixels
`<HR WIDTH="%">`	line's width as a percentage of the page width

Lists

Lists are ubiquitous in webpages, usually appearing as lists of target locations. They may be ordered (each item is preceded by a letter or number) or unordered (each item is preceded by a bullet point).

`<UL><LI></UL>`	unordered list (<LI> before each list item)
`<UL TYPE=DISC|CIRCLE|SQUARE>`	bullet type for the whole list
`<LI TYPE=DISC|CIRCLE|SQUARE>`	bullet type for this and subsequent items
`<OL><LI></OL>`	ordered list (<LI> before each list item)
`<OL TYPE=A|a|I|i|1>`	numbering type (for the whole list)
`<LI TYPE=A|a|I|i|1>`	numbering type (this and subsequent)
`<OL START=?>`	starting number (for the whole list)
`<LI VALUE=?>`	starting number (this and subsequent)
`<DL><DT><DD></DL>`	definition list (<DT>=term, <DD>=definition)
`<MENU><LI></MENU>`	menu list (<LI> before each list item)
`<DIR><LI></DIR>`	directory list (<LI> before each list item)

Colours and Backgrounds

Colours are defined by triplets of two-digit hexadecimal numbers that define the amount of red, green and blue in that colour. For example the triplet FF0000 defines pure red, FFFFFF defines white and 00FFFF defines red's complementary colour. We want to define a background colour for a page, the colour text should have, and the colours of unvisited links, visited links and active links (i.e. the colour the link takes as you click on it). These declarations must all appear in the head of the document.

`<BODY BGCOLOR="#$$$$$$">`	background colour
`<BODY TEXT="#$$$$$$">`	text colour
`<BODY LINK="#$$$$$$">`	link colour
`<BODY VLINK="#$$$$$$">`	visited link
`<BODY ALINK="#$$$$$$">`	active link

The background colours are set up in the document's header.

Forms

Forms provide a simple method of allowing a user to give feedback from a webpage, either freeform text or by selecting one of a set of options. Their use requires some script on the host to process the returned data.

`<FORM ACTION= "URL"` `METHOD=GET│POST> </FORM>`	defines a form

`<FORM ENCTYPE=`
`"multipart/form-`
`data></FORM>`
	form upload

`<INPUT TYPE="TEXT│`
`PASSWORD│CHECKBOX│RADIO│`
`IMAGE│HIDDEN│SUBMIT│`
`RESET">`
	input field

`<INPUT NAME="***">`	field name
`<INPUT VALUE="***">`	field value
`<INPUT CHECKED>`	is the field checked? (checkboxes and radio boxes)
`<INPUT SIZE=?>`	field size in characters
`<INPUT MAXLENGTH=?>`	maximum field length in characters
`<SELECT></SELECT>`	selection list
`<SELECT NAME="***">` `</SELECT>`	name of list
`<SELECT SIZE=?></SELECT>`	number of options
`<SELECT MULTIPLE>`	multiple choice allowed
`<OPTION>`	an option
`<OPTION SELECTED>`	the default option
`<TEXTAREA ROWS=?` `COLS=?></TEXTAREA>`	input box size
`<TEXTAREA NAME="***">` `</TEXTAREA>`	name of box

`<TEXTAREA WRAP=OFF│`
`VIRTUAL│PHYSICAL>`
`</TEXTAREA>`
	a wrap box

Tables

Used to organise arrays of data.

`<TABLE></TABLE>`	Define Table
`<TABLE BORDER></TABLE>`	Table Border (either on or off)
`<TABLE BORDER=?></TABLE>`	Table Border (you can set the value)
`<TABLE CELLSPACING=?>`	Cell Spacing
`<TABLE CELLPADDING=?>`	Cell Padding
`<TABLE WIDTH=?>`	Desired Width (in pixels)
`<TABLE WIDTH=%>`	Width Percent (percentage of page)
`<TR></TR>`	Table Row
`<TR ALIGN=LEFT|RIGHT| CENTER VALIGN=TOP| MIDDLE|BOTTOM>`	Alignment
`<TD></TD>`	Table Cell (must appear within table rows)
`<TD ALIGN=LEFT|RIGHT| CENTER VALIGN=TOP| MIDDLE|BOTTOM>`	Alignment
`<TD NOWRAP>`	No linebreaks
`<TD COLSPAN=?>`	Columns to Span
`<TD ROWSPAN=?>`	Rows to Span
`<TH></TH>`	Table Header (same as data, except bold centred)
`<TH ALIGN=LEFT|RIGHT| CENTER VALIGN=TOP| MIDDLE|BOTTOM>`	Alignment
`<TH NOWRAP>`	No Linebreaks
`<TH COLSPAN=?>`	Columns to Span
`<TH ROWSPAN=?>`	Rows to Span
`<CAPTION></CAPTION>`	Table Caption
`<CAPTION ALIGN=TOP| BOTTOM>`	Alignment (above/below table)

Frames

Define and manipulate specific regions of the window.

`<FRAMESET></FRAMESET>`	Define the Frame Document (instead of `<BODY>`)
`<FRAMESET ROWS=,,,> </FRAMESET>`	Row Heights (pixels or %)

`<FRAMESET ROWS=*>`	Row Heights (* = relative size)
`</FRAMESET>`	
`<FRAMESET COLS=,,,>`	Column Widths (pixels or %)
`</FRAMESET>`	
`<FRAMESET COLS=*>`	Column Widths (* = relative size)
`</FRAMESET>`	
`<FRAMESET`	Borders
`FRAMEBORDER="yes│no">`	
`<FRAMESET BORDER=?>`	Border Width
`<FRAMESET BORDERCOLOR=`	Border Colour
`"#$$$$$$">`	
`<FRAME>`	Define Frame (contents of an individual frame)
`<FRAME SRC="URL">`	Display Document
`<FRAME NAME=`	Frame Name
`"***"│_blank│_self│`	
`_parent│_top>`	
`<FRAME MARGINWIDTH=?>`	Margin Width (left and right margins)
`<FRAME MARGINHEIGHT=?>`	Margin Height (top and bottom margins)
`<FRAME SCROLLING="YES│`	Scrollbar? Default is AUTO, the browser will add scrollbars if needed
`NO│AUTO">`	
`<FRAME NORESIZE>`	Not Resizable
`<FRAME FRAMEBORDER=`	Borders
`"yes│no">`	
`<FRAME BORDERCOLOR=`	Border Colour
`"#$$$$$$">`	
`<NOFRAMES></NOFRAMES>`	Unframed Content (for non-frames browsers)

A framed page requires at least three files: one declares the structure of the frames and the HTML documents that will appear in each frame of the page. The other two or more files will contain the data to place in each frame. (You could make a framed page with just a single frame, this would only require the two files, but would not look any different to a normal web page!)

Java

These tags define how a Java applet is linked in to your web page.

`<APPLET></APPLET>`	Applet
`<APPLET CODE="***">`	File Name
`<APPLET PARAM NAME="***">`	Parameters
`<APPLET CODEBASE="URL">`	Location
`<APPLET NAME="***">`	Identifier (for references)
`<APPLET ALT="***">`	Alt Text (for non-Java browsers)
`<APPLET ALIGN="LEFT| RIGHT|CENTER">`	Alignment
`<APPLET WIDTH=? HEIGHT=?>`	Size (in pixels)
`<APPLET HSPACE=? VSPACE=?>`	Spacing (in pixels)

The applet to be linked will have been written in one of two ways. The basic approach is to write the Java code using a simple word-processor. The code (a *.java) file will have been translated to the Java bytecode using javac, the Java compiler. The Java software development kit (SDK) is available free of charge from Sun Microcomputers. The less basic method of creating the applet is using an integrated programming environment, many are available. The java source file will have been compiled to a java class, a file of the same name but the extension .class, this is linked into the web page.

Miscellaneous

These are odd tags that do not fit in to any of the above sections.

`<!– *** –>`	Comment (not displayed by the browser)
`<!DOCTYPE HTML PUBLIC "-//W3C//DTD HTML 3.2//EN">`	Prologue
`<ISINDEX>`	Searchable (indicates a searchable index)
`<ISINDEX PROMPT="***">`	Prompt (text to prompt input)
`<A HREF="URL?***"></a>`	Send Search (use a real question mark)
`<BASE HREF="URL">`	URL of This File (must be in header)
`<BASE TARGET="***">`	Base Window Name (must be in header)
`<LINK REV="***" REL="***" HREF="URL">`	Relationship (in header)

`<META>`	Meta Information (must be in header)
`<STYLE></STYLE>`	Style Sheets (not widely supported yet)
`<SCRIPT></SCRIPT>`	Scripts (not widely supported yet)

With this information, you should be able to start designing your own web pages. The easiest way is to experiment and learn for yourself what is possible and how it can be achieved.

Bibliography

Raggett D, Lam J, Alexander I, Kmiec M (1998) *Raggett on HTML 4.0*, Addison–Wesley, Harlow.

Appendix 2
Mathematical Techniques

Introduction

Several of the book's chapters introduced new mathematical techniques. At the time, the purpose of each technique was explained, but the theory was omitted. This appendix summarises the theoretical background to these techniques.

Discrete Cosine Transform

The Fourier transform yields a description of the frequency content of a signal, either a speech signal or an image. Sounds of short duration or small objects will have a frequency content that covers a wider range of frequency components than large objects or sounds of a longer duration. By the nature of their sampling properties, the frequency content of digitised signals will be concentrated towards the lower frequency ranges. Thus, if an image or a speech signal is Fourier transformed, the higher frequency components will have negligibly small values, most of the information content of the signal will be in the lower frequency components. The high frequency components will contain information about the fine scale structure of the data, e.g. edges in images.

The Fourier transform can be computed by multiplying each element of a signal by the appropriate weights and summing the results. The weights are derived from sine and cosine functions. The discrete cosine transformation uses only the cosine terms of the Fourier transform, and provides a method of organising the data in a signal such that the most significant contributions appear in the lower entries. As far as signal coding is concerned this is useful, as we may retain coefficients whose values are above some threshold and set the remainder to zero. This data would be represented as the finite coefficients, the number of zeroes would be inferred.

The discrete cosine transform is defined as:

$$X(u) = \sum_{n=0}^{n=N-1} x(n) \cos\left(\frac{(2n+1)\pi u}{2N}\right)$$

Short Term Fourier Transform

The discrete Fourier transform is defined by:

$$X(u) = \sum_{n=-\infty}^{n=\infty} x(n) \exp\left(-\frac{2\pi nu}{f}\right)$$

Note that the limits of the summation extend over the entire range of input data.

There are many properties of the transform to be taken into account as it is used, one that is relevant in this application stems from the convolution theorem. The convolution theorem states that if two signals are multiplied together, the result is identical to what is obtained by convolving their Fourier transforms; and equivalently, if two signals are convolved together, then the result is identical to what is obtained by taking the product of their transforms.

This is applicable if an infinitely long signal is windowed, that is, its values are set to zero outside some range by multiplying it by a windowing function:

$$W_n = \begin{cases} 1 \\ 0 \end{cases} \quad 0 \leqslant n \leqslant N$$

We therefore expect the transform of the windowed function to look like the transform of the original convolved with the transform of the windowing function. Figure A2.1 illustrates this by showing an infinite and a windowed signal and their Fourier transforms. The effect of windowing is to obscure the required transform information.

An alternative way of viewing windowing is that it introduces discontinuities to the data, Figure A2.1b demonstrates that at the window boundaries, the signal becomes discontinuous, i.e. there is an immediate change from a finite value to zero. The discontinuities contribute to the transform by obscuring the required detail.

One method of resolving this problem is to force the signal data to taper to zero at its ends. This reduces the magnitude of the discontinuities and hence reduces their obscuring effect. One common windowing function (in speech processing) is the Hamming window, defined by:

$$W_n = \begin{cases} 0.54 + 0.46 \cos\left(\dfrac{2\pi n}{N-1}\right) \\ 0 \end{cases} \quad 0 \leqslant n \leqslant N$$

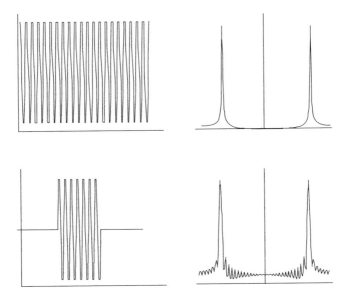

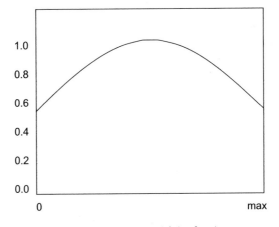

Figure A2.1 Continuous and windowed functions (left) and their Fourier transforms (right)

Figure A2.2 The Hamming weighting function

The function is plotted in Figure A2.2, and its effect on the transformation is shown in Figure A2.3, in which the same data as in Figure A2.1 has been weighted with the Hamming window and transformed. The expected structure is much more apparent because the artefacts introduced by the discontinuities have been reduced.

The short term Fourier transform can now be defined. A set of N samples of the data are abstracted. They are weighted with the Hamming window and passed through the Fourier transform. The following N

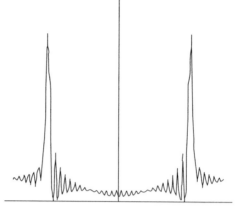

Figure A2.3 Hamming weighted data and its Fourier transform

samples are then transformed. Once completed, the short term Fourier transform demonstrates the temporal development of the signal's frequency components.

Edge Detection

Edges are extremely important structures in images as they define the outlines of objects and the boundaries of regions. In the context of the eye-mouse or head-joystick, the face outline, the borders of facial features and other objects are defined by edges.

An edge may be defined as a significant, local difference in image brightness. Therefore we will observe very different image values on either side of the edge and the pixels having these values will have a small separation. Edge detectors work by increasing this difference (edge enhancement) and subsequently searching for large difference values (thresholding).

Edge enhancement is usually achieved by differentiating the image. It is helpful to think of the image as a landscape. Edges then correspond to hillsides, the more significant the edge, the steeper the hillside. The process of edge detection results in a line being drawn across a hillside that links adjacent points of maximum slope. (This analogy also illustrates one of the absurdities of edge detection: it attempts to define a line that localises the edge when in reality the edge exists over the entire slope.)

Since the image is a two dimensional structure, it must be differentiated in two orthogonal directions, those parallel to the image sides are usually chosen, though other directions have been used. Differentiation can be achieved by differencing pairs of neighbouring pixels. Following the hillside analogy, this is equivalent to measuring the height differences between two pairs of points at a fixed horizontal separation, one pair has a north to south alignment and the other an east to west alignment.

Having differentiated the image, we have estimates of the strength of the edge in two directions, we need the absolute edge strength, or slope of the hillside. This is computed by combining the edge strength measures in quadrature (that is, taking the square root of the sum of their squared values). A less accurate, but computationally quicker estimate of edge strength is obtained by adding the absolute values of the edge strengths.

The final step of edge detection is to threshold the edge strength measures. This is equivalent to supposing that edge strengths below some value are insignificantly small. This introduces many errors to the edge detection process, most significantly it removes small but significant edges, which must be reinstated at some later stage of the processing.

Recently, optimal edge detectors have been suggested. These attempt to locate edges under some optimality criteria. For example, Canny's detector was designed to give a single response to a step edge that was corrupted by additive noise. The Canny operator is realised by convolving the data with the two templates generated from:

$$t_x(x, y) = xe^{-\frac{2\pi x^2}{\sigma^2}}$$

$$t_y(x, y) = ye^{-\frac{2\pi y^2}{\sigma^2}}$$

By choosing different values of σ, edges of differing spatial extents may be detected. Large values will have the effect of smoothing small scale edges, leaving larger scale edges.

Hough Transform

The Hough transform was patented in 1962 as an algorithm to locate lines in images. The starting point in its derivation is to remember that the equation of a straight line can be written as:

$$y = mx + c$$

Where x and y are coordinates of points on the line, m is the line's gradient and c is the point at which the line crosses the vertical (y) axis. If we had a point in the image, then an infinite number of lines could be drawn through it, each would have a unique pair of m and c values. We could represent these combinations of values as a line in a c-m graph whose equation can be derived by rearranging the line's equation:

$$m = -\frac{c}{x} + \frac{y}{x}$$

This is recognisable as a straight line, having a gradient of $-1/x$ and an intercept of y/x. The line is drawn by computing the m value for each value of c using the x and y values of the point we have.

If a second point is found in the image, it too may be transformed into a line in the c-m graph. It will be a different line, but there will be a point of intersection of the two lines. The values of c and m at this intersection will fix the line passing through the two image points. As more image points are transformed into lines in the c-m graph, we will gather evidence for the linear structures in the image, they will be defined by c-m combinations where multiple transform lines intersect.

The Hough transform is implemented by making the c-m graph an array of accumulator cells. Each cell is addressed by a unique c-m combination and its contents record the number of points that have contributed to this combination. The Hough transform itself takes each image point and computes the c-m combinations of the lines that could pass through it. The contents of these cells are incremented. Finally the array is inspected for local maxima, the c and m values of the cells whose values are local maxima define the equations of lines in the original image. No information can be obtained regarding the endpoints of the lines.

The Hough transform is usually used for finding the outlines of objects in an image. The points we want as its input are therefore to be found on the boundaries of objects where there is a sharp local change in image brightness. The points can be found by differentiating the image and thresholding the results, as was explained above.

A major problem with this specific implementation is that c and m values can become extremely large. To overcome this, a slightly different line equation is used which represents the line using its minimum distance from the origin and the angle it makes with the positive x axis.

Finally, versions of the Hough transform have been defined for other analytically defined shapes, circles and ellipses were used in Chapter 8, and also for arbitrary shapes.

Appendix 3
Publicly Available Software

Introduction

Many tools are required when developing multimedia systems, whether they be information presentation systems or information processing systems. The purpose of this Appendix is to list some of the public domain or free evaluation tools that can be readily accessed.

Please note that inclusion of a product in this appendix does not imply that it is suitable for any particular purpose nor does it imply my endorsement.

Multimedia Authoring Tools

Authoring tools allow presentations to be constructed easily by orchestrating the appearances of the presentation's components.

Macromedia

An evaluation version of Macromedia's multimedia authoring tool, Director, is available from their website: http://www.macromedia.com/software/director. Being an evaluation copy, certain functions are disabled.

Other Tools

Locations of other tools may be found in the comp.multimedia newsgroup's FAQ.

Image Processing Software

These are packages intended for scientific processing of images and short sequences of images. Nevertheless, they are very powerful packages that can be very useful when preparing images for inclusion in a presentation.

NIH Image and Image-J

NIH Image was developed at the National Institute of Health. It is a Macintosh based package and includes a very extensive library of image processing routines. A PC based version of the same programme is also available.

Image website: zippy.nimh.nih.gov/pub/nih-image/

PC-Image website: http://www.scioncorp.com/index.htm

Development of Image ceased some years ago, when a Java version was released. Being platform independent, this version can be executed on the Mac, the PC and all UNIX machines.

Image-J website: http://rsb.info.nih.gov/ij/

ImageTool

ImageTool was developed in the School of Dentistry in the University of Texas. If performs many of the functions of NIH-Image, but is PC based. It also includes support for the TWAIN scanner interface and a video capture card.

ImageTool website: http://macorb.uthscsa.edu/dig/itdesc.html

Image Editing Software

The above programmes were intended for scientific work, the following programmes are general purpose image manipulation packages.

Graphic Converter

Graphic Converter is a shareware package for the Macintosh. It allows images to be translated between numerous formats.

Graphic converter website: http://www.lemkesoft.de/

PhotoShop

PhotoShop is a shareware image manipulation package. It is available at numerous archives, and also appears frequently on computer magazine's cover disks.

Freehand

Freehand is a professional quality drawing package. An evaluation copy is available from Macromedia: www.macromedia.com.

Video Processing Software

Microsoft have developed a Vision Software Development Kit that contains drivers and example software to capture and store images from any Video For Windows compatible device, such as Creative Lab's VideoBlaster.

Microsoft Vision SDK: http://www.research.microsoft.com/vision/

Pong Suvan has developed a video and image processing package. It takes input from a data file (either an image or a sequence) or from a Video for Windows (VfW) compatible device. Rudimentary processing functions are provided, but the package is extensible, the user is able to create specific filters that achieve data processing tasks.

Two versions have been developed, one takes input from files or a VfW device, the other only from a VfW device.

http://www.ccs.neu.edu/home/psksvp

Video Editing Software

Ulead market image and video editing software that is frequently bundled with graphics cards: www.ulead.com

Sound Editing Software

Many sound manipulation programs are listed at the comp.speech FAQ site. One of the more useful shareware programs is Goldwave: http://www. goldwave.com/

Link Sites

Several topic specific archive sites exist that contain information pertinent to this software. It is likely that these sites will be longer lived than many of the package specific sites.

Computer Vision Homepage:
http://www.cs.cmu.edu/afs/cs/project/cil/ftp/html/vision.html

Efg's Image Processing Page:
http://www.efg2.com/lab/library/ImageProcessing/
SoftwarePackages.htm

Comp.speech FAQ: http://svr-www.eng.cam.ac.uk/comp.speech

Other links are maintained in the FAQ associated with the comp.multimedia newsgroup.

Index